A PORTRAIT OF HUMANKIND

Current Readings in

Physical Anthropology

Edited by
Arthur Charles Durband
and Robert Rolfe Paine
Texas Tech University, Lubbock

cognella™
San Diego, CA

First published in the United States of America in 2011 by Cognella, a division of University Readers, Inc.

Trademark Notice: Product or corporate names may be trademarks or registered trademarks, and are used only for identification and explanation without intent to infringe.

15 14 13 12 11   1 2 3 4 5

Printed in the United States of America

ISBN: 978-1-60927-022-3

www.cognella.com   800.200.3908

Contents

Chapter 5: Human Variation   95

Chapter 1

Genetics and Evolutionary Theory

Genetics is a cornerstone to the study of biology and our understanding of evolutionary principles. Advances in human genetic research are coming faster than most non-scientists can keep by with. Whether we realize it or not this science is impacting our lives. Medical research, cloning of body parts, producing new/genetically altered foods use for animal and human consumption are just a few examples of how these new insights into genes affects us. How can we better understand the consequences of using this technology? It can happen successfully only if we are educated in basic facts of the sciences.

Unfortunately, there is a perception among many Americans today that evolution is "just a theory" and is still questioned by scientists. Misinformation and pseudoscience like "intelligent design" have been proposed as alternatives, even though these ideas are not scientific. Contrary to some corners of popular opinion, evolution is a very strong theory backed by over 150 years of research that has undergone considerable peer review. An understanding of evolution is crucial for the application of new information revealed by genetic studies.

As you may have seen on many television shows, the study of genetics has changed how we solve crimes. Human DNA is now used to convict criminals of a wide range of crimes. It has also been used to show that some folks have been incorrectly convicted of a crime. CSI shows make this look easy and fool proof. Still, such cases are judged by jurors, people like you. If you found yourself in that situation, would you prefer to have jurors that have a college education and a basic understanding of biology and genetics, or others that have barely made through high school biology? Each of us has a responsibility to understand how genetics works and is applied. The following articles help to bring these points into focus.

A Fin Is a Limb Is a Wing

How Evolution Fashioned Its Masterworks

By Carl Zimmer

Eyes, wings, elaborate bodies—nature is filled with breathtakingly complex structures. Now scientists are learning how they emerged. From minute sea creatures to insects to humans, the same body-building genes are at work, revealing evolution's path from simple beginnings to intricate forms.

The father of evolution was a nervous parent. Few things worried Charles Darwin more than the challenge of explaining how nature's most complex structures, such as the eye, came to be. "The eye to this day gives me a cold shudder," he wrote to a friend in 1860.

Today biologists are beginning to understand the origins of life's complexity—the exquisite optical mechanism of the eye, the masterly engineering of the arm, the architecture of a flower or a feather, the choreography that allows trillions of cells to cooperate in a single organism.

The fundamental answer is clear: In one way or another, all these wonders evolved. "The basic idea of evolution is so elegant, so beautiful, so simple," says Howard Berg, a Harvard researcher who has spent much of the past 40 years studying one of the humbler examples of nature's complexity, the spinning tail of common bacteria. "The idea is simply that you fiddle around and you change something and then you ask, Does it improve my survival or not? And if it doesn't, then those individuals die

and that idea goes away. And if it does, then those individuals succeed, and you keep fiddling around, improving. It's an enormously powerful technique."

But nearly 150 years after Darwin first brought this elegant idea to the world's attention when he published *The Origin of Species,* the evolution of complex structures can still be hard to accept. Most of us can envision natural selection tweaking a simple trait—making an animal furrier, for example, or its neck longer. Yet it's harder to picture evolution producing a new complex organ, complete with all its precisely interlocking parts. Creationists claim that life is so complex that it could not have evolved. They often cite the virtuoso engineering of the bacterial tail, which resembles a tiny electric motor spinning a shaft, to argue that such complexity must be the direct product of "intelligent design" by a superior being.

The vast majority of biologists do not share this belief. Studying how complex structures came to be is one of the most exciting frontiers in evolutionary biology, with clues coming at remarkable speed.

Some have emerged from spectacular fossils that reveal the precursors of complex organs such as limbs or feathers. Others come from laboratories, where scientists are studying the genes that turn featureless embryos into mature organisms. By comparing the genes that build bodies in different species, they've found evidence that structures as seemingly different as the eyes of a fly and a human being actually have a shared heritage.

The underside of a mantid reveals the complex structures that evolution added to its simpler ancestors: compound eyes, bristled limbs, two kinds of wings. Scientists are finding that all these structures have deep roots. The same genes that build them in a mantid are turning up—often doing different jobs—in less elaborate creatures.

Scientists still have a long way to go in understanding the evolution of complexity, which isn't surprising since many of life's devices evolved hundreds of millions of years ago. Nevertheless, new discoveries are revealing the steps by which complex structures developed from simple beginnings. Through it all, scientists keep rediscovering a few key rules. One is that a complex structure can evolve through a series of simpler intermediates. Another is that nature is thrifty, modifying old genes for new uses and even reusing the same genes in new ways, to build something more elaborate.

Sean Carroll, a biologist at the University of Wisconsin-Madison, likens the body-building genes to construction workers. "If you walked past a construction site at 6 p.m. every day, you'd say, Wow, it's a miracle—the building is building itself. But if you sat there all day and saw the workers and the tools, you'd understand how it was put together. We can now see the workers and the machinery. And the same machinery and workers can build any structure."

A limb, a feather, or a flower is a marvel, but not a miracle.

From One Cell to Trillions

In every human body roughly ten trillion cells—brainless units of life—come together to work as a unified whole. "It's a complex dance," says Nicole King, a biologist at the University of California, Berkeley, requiring organization and constant communication. And it began more than 600 million years ago when organisms containing just one cell gave rise to the first multicellular animals, the group that now includes creatures as diverse as sea sponges, beetles, and us. It turns out that some of those single-celled ancestors were already equipped for social life.

King studies some of our closest living single-celled relatives, known as choanoflagellates. Choanoflagellates are easy to find. Just scoop some water from a local creek or marsh, put a few drops under a microscope, and you may see the tadpole-shaped creatures flitting about. You can tell them apart from other protozoans by a distinctive collar at the base of their tail.

When King and her colleagues examined the proteins made by choanoflagellates, they found several that were thought to be unique to animals—molecules essential to maintaining a multicellular body. "It really blew our minds," says King. "What are these single-celled organisms doing with these proteins?"

Some of the proteins normally create what King calls "an armlock between cells," keeping animal cells from sticking together randomly. King and her colleagues are running experiments to figure out how choanoflagellates use these adhesive proteins—perhaps to snag bacteria for food. Others play a role in cell-to-cell communication. Choanoflagellates, which presumably have no need to talk to other cells, may use these proteins to sense changes in their environment.

The discoveries suggest that many of the tools necessary to build a multicellular body already existed in our single-celled ancestors. Evolution borrowed those tools for a new task: building bodies of increasing complexity.

Blueprints for Bodies

A developing fly larva looks as featureless as a grain of rice. But it already bears a map of the complex creature it will become. Across the larva, different combinations of genes are active, marking it off into invisible compartments. These genes turn on other genes that give each compartment its shape and function: Some sprout legs, others wings, others antennae. An invisible anatomy becomes visible.

Flies aren't the only animals that build their bodies this way. Scientists have found that the genes responsible for laying out the fly's body plan have nearly identical counterparts in many other animals, ranging from crabs to earthworms to lampreys to us. The discovery came as a surprise, since these animals have such different-looking bodies. But now scientists generally agree that the common ancestor of all these animals— a wormlike creature that lived an estimated 570 million years ago—already had a basic set of body-plan genes. Its descendants then used those genes to build new kinds of bodies.

To appreciate how this tool kit can generate complexity, consider the velvet worm. The velvet worm creeps along the floors of tropical forests on nearly identical pad-shaped legs. It is, frankly, a boring little creature. Yet it is also the closest living relative to the single most diverse group of animals, the arthropods. Among arthropods, you can find a dizzying range of complex bodies, from butterflies to tarantulas, horseshoe crabs, ticks, and lobsters.

Scientists studying body-plan genes think arthropods started out much like velvet worms,

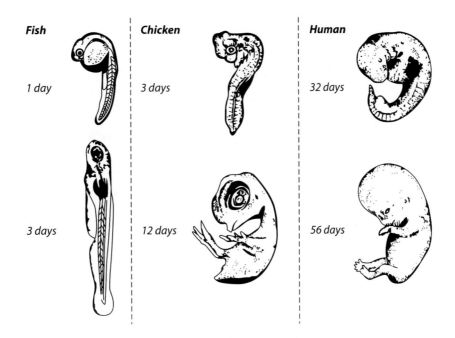

TAKING SHAPE *An animal's complex adult form emerges as its embryo develops. The early embryos of three different vertebrates—a fish, a chicken, and a human—look much the same. But genes active in corresponding parts of the embryos (red) guide development down different paths, producing a fin, a wing, or an arm. Evolution often reshapes organisms by tinkering with the genes that control development.*

Choanoflagellate

The animal kingdom dates back more than 600 million years, to when single-celled creatures—microscopic, water-sifting sacs propelled by undulating filaments—gave rise to many-celled animals like sponges and other marine invertebrates (yellow and orange masses, right). The fragile organisms that made this transition left no fossils, so scientists study choanoflagellates (illustrated above, with red food particles), perhaps the closest living one-celled relatives of animals. Even though they are solitary cells, choanoflagellates turn out to have genes that make proteins essential to multicellular life. This suggests that the one-celled ancestors of all animals were genetically equipped for "animalhood," although they put those tools to other uses.

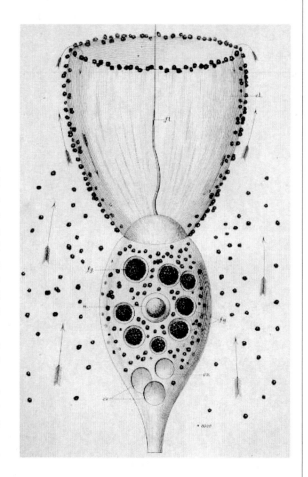

using the same basic set of body-building genes to lay out their anatomy. Over time, copies of those genes began to be borrowed for new jobs. The invisible map of the arthropod body plan became more complex, with more compartments and new body parts sprouting from them.

Some compartments, for example, developed organs for breathing; later, in insects, those breathing organs evolved into wings. Early insect fossils preserve wings sprouting from many segments. Over time, insects shut off the wing-building genes in all but a few segments—or used some of the same genes to build new structures. Flies, for example, have just one pair of wings; a second pair has turned into club-shaped structures called halteres, which help flies stay balanced in flight.

"The segments have all become different, the appendages have all become different, but the machinery for making appendages is the same," says Sean Carroll. "Evolution is a tinkerer, an improviser."

How We Got a Head

The human head is, inch for inch, the most complex part of our body. Not only does it contain our brain, but it also packs in most of our sense organs: eyes, ears, a nose, and a tongue. The intricate bones of the skull add to the head's complexity, from the cranium that keeps the brain safe to the jaws that allow us to eat. Thousands of variations on the theme

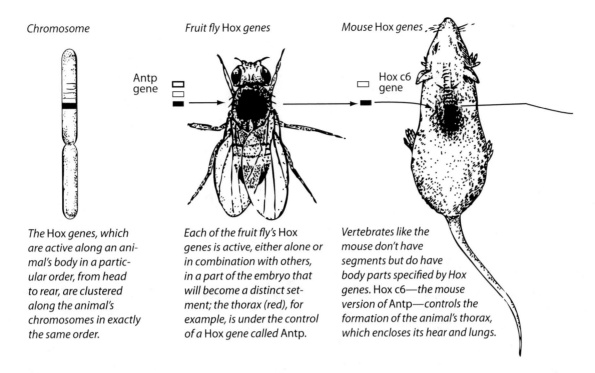

Chromosome

Fruit fly Hox genes

Mouse Hox genes

Antp gene

Hox c6 gene

The Hox genes, which are active along an animal's body in a particular order, from head to rear, are clustered along the animal's chromosomes in exactly the same order.

Each of the fruit fly's Hox genes is active, either alone or in combination with others, in a part of the embryo that will become a distinct set-ment; the thorax (red), for example, is under the control of a Hox gene called Antp.

Vertebrates like the mouse don't have segments but do have body parts specified by Hox genes. Hox c6—the mouse version of Antp—controls the formation of the animal's thorax, which encloses its hear and lungs.

SAME MASTER GENES Hox *genes act as master switches, turning on sets of other genes that guide the formation of distinct regions of an animal's body. Species from flies to mice to people all have inherited their* Hox *genes from a common ancestor.*

exist—think of hammerhead sharks, of anteaters, of toucans.

All those heads become even more remarkable when you look at two simple sea creatures that are the closest living relatives of the vertebrates (animals with backbones). These humble organisms have no heads at all. But they have the makings of one in their genes.

The larvacean, a tiny gelatinous tadpole, lives in a floating house it builds with its own mucus. Its nervous system, such as it is, is organized around a simple nerve cord running along its back. Even stranger is its cousin, the sea squirt. It starts out as a swimming larva, with a rodlike stiffener in its tail. When it matures, it drives its front end into the ocean floor, eats most of its nervous system, and turns its body into a basket for filtering food particles.

At first glance, these creatures seem unlikely to hold any clues to the origin of the vertebrate head. But a close look at the front tip of larvaceans and larval sea squirts reveals a small brainlike organ where a vertebrate would have a head. "There are 360 neural cells there. Compared with the vertebrate brain, that's nothing," says William Jeffery, a biologist at the University of Maryland. Yet scientists have seen

a strikingly familiar pattern in how that tiny cluster of cells develops. Some of the same genes that build our own brains are at work there, and in roughly the same areas—front, middle, and rear.

Jeffery and his colleagues have also found that sea squirts have what appear to be primitive cousins of neural crest cells—the kind of cells that build much of the head in the developing embryos of vertebrates. Like our own neural crest cells, the sea squirt's emerge along the back of the developing embryo and migrate through the body. But instead of making a skull, neurons, and other parts of the head, they turn into pigment cells, adding brilliant colors to sea squirt bodies.

Over half a billion years ago our own headless ancestors may have resembled these modest creatures, already equipped with genes and cells that would later sculpt the faces and brains that make us human.

Catching the Light

Charles Darwin was well acquainted with the exquisite construction of the eye—the way the lens is

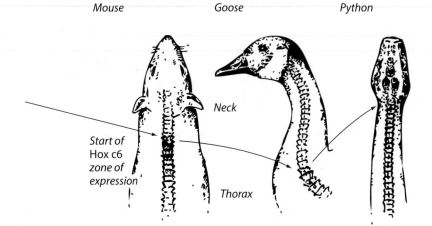

Mouse   Goose   Python

Neck

*Start of
Hox c6
zone of
expression*

Thorax

MANY VARIATIONS *Body proportions can change depending on where particular* Hox *genes are active. The same* Hox *gene,* Hox c6, *switches on at different points along the body. Since that gene marks the beginning of the thorax, different species end up with necks of varying lengths—a short neck in the mouse, a long one in the goose, and in the python, no neck at all.*

perfectly positioned to focus light onto the retina, the way the iris adjusts the amount of light that enters the eye. An eye, it seemed, would be useless if it were anything less than perfect. In *The Origin of Species,* Darwin wrote that the idea of natural selection producing the eye "seems, I freely confess, absurd in the highest degree."

Yet the eye is actually far from perfect. The retina is so loosely attached to the back of the eye in humans that a sharp punch to the head may be enough to detach it. Its light-gathering cells point inward, toward the brain, not out toward the light. And the optic nerve starts out in front of the retina and then plunges through it to go to the brain. The place where the optic nerve burrows through the retina becomes the eye's blind spot. Evolution, with all its blunders, made the eye; Darwin himself had no doubt about that. But how?

A full answer has to account for not just our own eye, but all the eyes in the animal kingdom. Not long ago, the evidence suggested that the eyes in different kinds of animals—insects, cats, and octopuses, for example—must have evolved independently, much as wings evolved independently in birds and bats. After all, the differences between, say, a human eye and a fly's are profound. Unlike the human eye with its single lens and retina, the fly's is made up of thousands of tiny columns, each capturing a tiny fraction of the insect's field of

vision. And while we vertebrates capture light with cells known as ciliary photoreceptors (for their hairlike projections, called cilia), insects and other invertebrates use rhabdomeric photoreceptors, cells with distinctive folds.

In recent years, however, these differences became less stark as scientists examined the genes that build photoreceptors. Insects and humans use the same genes to tell cells in their embryos to turn into photoreceptors. And both kinds of photoreceptors snag light with molecules known as opsins.

These links suggested that photoreceptors in flies, humans, and most other animals all evolved from a single type of cell that eventually split into two new cell types. If so, some animals might carry both types of photoreceptors. And in 2004, scientists showed that rag worms, aquatic relatives of earthworms, have rhabdomeric photoreceptors in their eyes and ciliary photoreceptors hidden in their tiny brain, where they appear to sense light to set the rag worm's internal clock.

With such discoveries, a new picture of eye evolution is emerging. The common ancestor of most animals had a basic tool kit of genes for building organs that could detect light. These earliest eyes were probably much like those found today in little gelatinous sea creatures like salps: just pits lined with photoreceptor cells, adequate to sense light and tell its direction. Yet they were the handiwork of the

Horseshoe Crab

They've got legs—lots of them. Arthropods, the hard-shelled group including some 80 percent of all living animals, from insects to crabs, have been well endowed with limbs for hundreds of millions of years. But while millipedes (left) have a chain of trunk segments with nearly identical pairs of walking legs, a horseshoe crab (below) is a Swiss army knife of jointed limbs—for walking, swimming, grasping, shredding, and defending. Yet the same ancient cluster of Hox genes governs the development of body segments in all arthropods. What type of limbs a segment acquires depends on which Hox gene is in control there, and on how evolution has reshaped the original unadorned parts to suit new needs.

same genes that build our own eyes, and they relied on the same light-sensing opsins.

Evolution then used those basic genes to fashion more sophisticated eyes, which eventually acquired a lens for turning light into an image. The lens too did not appear out of nothing. Lenses are made of transparent proteins called crystallins, which can bend light "like protein glass," as one scientist says. And crystallins, it turns out, existed well before evolution put them to work in the eye. They were just doing other jobs.

Scientists have discovered one crystallin, for example, in the central nervous system of sea squirts. Instead of making a lens, it is part of a gravity-sensing organ. A mutation may have caused cells in the early vertebrate eye to make the crystallin as well. There it turned out to do something new and extraordinarily useful: bring the world into focus.

From Fins to Limbs

Look at your arms holding this magazine. They are marvels of complexity, containing dozens of finely sculpted bones linked by tendons and muscles, supplied with blood by a mesh of arteries, controlled by an intricate network of neurons, and snugly wrapped in skin. Until about 380 million years ago, such limbs did not exist. Today they can be found not just on humans reading magazines, but also on bats flying out of Arizona caves, horses galloping across Mongolian steppes, moles burrowing through Connecticut gardens, and whales diving thousands of feet in the Pacific Ocean.

Fossils and embryos have provided a wealth of clues to the evolution of limbs. And they tell much the same story. "The limb was assembled over evolutionary time," says Neil Shubin, a paleontologist at the University of Chicago. "It didn't appear in one fell swoop."

About 400 million years ago, a new lineage of fish called lobe-fins emerged, bearing the first glimmers of a limb. From the outside, lobe-fins looked like any other fish, with fins for swimming. But the bones inside their fins were larger and more heavily muscled than in other fish.

Over tens of millions of years, new lineages of lobe-fins evolved, and true limbs took shape. *Eusthenopteron*, a 385-million-year-old fish found in Canada, had fins that contained one large

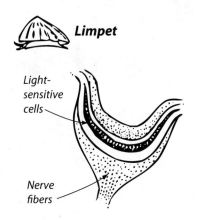

Limpet

Light-sensitive cells

Nerve fibers

Protected by a layer of transparent cells, this basic eye cannot form an image but sense light with photosensitive cells.

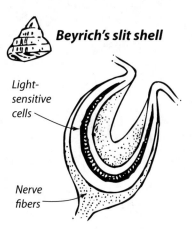

Beyrich's slit shell

Light-sensitive cells

Nerve fibers

A deeper eyecup provides more information about the direction of the light source, but creates no image.

EVOLUTION OF THE EYE *Scientists once thought that eyes evolved independently many times. Research now indicates that some of the eye-building genes evolved only once in an ancient animal. Evolution brought other genes under the control of these primordial eye genes, and together they produced eyes from simple to complex, such as these eyes from different species of mollusks.*

rod-shaped bone linked to a pair of smaller bones—the same pattern of long bones now found in our arms and legs. *Tiktaalik roseae*, a 375-million-year-old lobe-fin that Shubin and his colleagues recently discovered in northern Canada, added wrist and ankle bones. The scientists think *Tiktaalik* used its fins not only to swim but also to crawl across coastal wetlands.

"It's pushing up and pushing forward," says Shubin. "Could it walk? Could it rotate its shoulder and the rest? No. It's doing half the function, but it's half the function that suits the animal fully well."

By 365 million years ago, lobe-fins had given rise to vertebrates with true limbs, known as tetrapods, meaning four feet. These tetrapods even had toes, although they were still adapted to the water, retaining the gill bones of their ancestors and finned tails for swimming. Land walkers evolved later. And later still, tetrapods took the basic plan of the limb and adapted it to new functions—digging, paddling, and flying.

Laboratories are uncovering the genes responsible for building limbs and finding that once again, evolution used the tools already at hand: versions of the same genes that lay out animals' body plans. Once these genes mark off our bodies from head to tail, they become active in the tiny buds that become our arms and legs. Evolution must have borrowed these genes in early fish and reused them to build fins. Later, subtle shifts in the patterns formed by these genes caused these appendages to change shape into legs, arms, wings. Each transformation was profound. But, Shubin says, "you already had the machinery in place."

A Feather's Tale

As a feat of engineering, it's hard to beat the flight feather of a bird. From a central vane sprout hundreds of filaments called barbs. The barbs in turn sprout other, smaller filaments, some with grooves and some with hooks that zip the barbs together like Velcro. They create a lightweight plane that can lift a bird into the sky. When birds pull their feathers apart to clean them, the barbs simply zip back together by themselves.

Feathers do other jobs too. The club-winged manakin, a sparrow-size bird from the jungles of Ecuador, can rattle its wing feathers so loudly they sing. Owl feathers are a kind of natural stealth technology, dampening sound so that the birds can surprise their prey. Fuzzy down feathers keep birds warm, while extravagantly curved feathers attract mates. Yet all these complex structures share their origins with prosaic reptile scales—a journey that Richard Prum, an ornithologist at Yale, is tracing.

The evolutionary link between feathers and scales is obvious on developing bird embryos. Disks

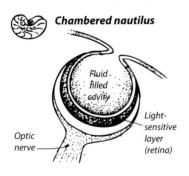

A small gap at the top of the eye chamber acts as a pinhole pupil that focuses light on a rudimentary retina to form a dim image.

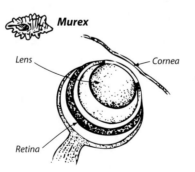

Fluid in a fully enclosed eye cavity functions as a primitive lens, focusing light on the retina to create a slightly sharper image.

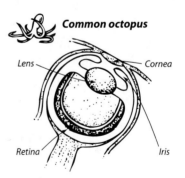

Advanced vision is delivered by a complex eye equipped with protective cornea, colored iris, and focusing lens.

Sources: Michael F. Landand, Dan Eric Nilsson, *Animal Eyes*, Monroe W. Strickberger, *Evolution*. Art by John Burgoyne

of cells called placodes are scattered across the surface of the embryo. Some grow into scales, such as the ones that cover a chicken's legs. Others turn into feathers.

Prum's research indicates that feathers evolved in a series of steps, with old genes being borrowed each time for new uses. In reptile embryos specific genes mark off the front and back of each scale as it grows from a placode. In bird embryos, each feather begins as a tube growing from a placode, and the same front and back genes are at work in the tube. Some 150 million years ago, says Prum, those genes must have taken on this new role in dinosaurs, causing some to sprout the feathers and feather-like growths that recent fossil finds have revealed.

The appearance of branch-like barbs was the next step in feather evolution, Prum argues, and the development of a baby bird's downy feathers offers clues to how that happened. As a new feather tube grows, it divides into strips, which eventually peel away into barbs. And once again, only a little tinkering with genes may have been required to get the tube to split. Prum has shown that the same genes that mark the front and back of reptile scales and feather tubes also mark the points around the tube where it will split.

Later, birds evolved the ability to turn these fluffy feathers into feathers with vanes, and then to lock the barbs together to make flight feathers, all with slight genetic changes that Prum is tracing. And by tweaking the growth of different parts of the feather, birds evolved special plumage for hunting, swimming, courting, and other activities, Prum says. "All the kinds of stuff that the bird needs throughout its life, it can generate with the same basic information."

Early Blooming

Like many other Victorian gentlemen, Charles Darwin was fond of plants. He packed his hothouses with sundews, cowslips, and Venus flytraps. He had exotic orchids shipped from the tropics. And yet, as he wrote to a friend in 1879, flowers were for him "an abominable mystery."

Darwin was referring to the sudden, unheralded emergence of flowers in the fossil record. Making the mystery all the more abominable was the exquisite complexity of flowers. Typical flowers have whorls of petals and petal-shaped sepals surrounding the plant's male and female sex organs. Many also produce brilliant pigments and sweet nectars to lure insects, which ferry pollen from flower to flower.

Today the mystery of flowers is less abominable, although big questions still remain. The first flowers must have evolved after the ancestors of flowering plants split from their closest living relatives, the gymnosperms—including pines and other conifers, cycads, and ginkgoes—which produce seeds but not flowers.

Some of the most important clues to this transition come from the genes active each time a plant blossoms. It turns out that before a flower takes shape, sets of genes mark out an invisible map at the tip of the stem—the same kind of map found on animal embryos.

The genes divide the tip into concentric rings. "It's like a stack of doughnuts on top of the stem," says Vivian Irish of Yale. Guided by the genes, cells in each ring develop into different flower parts—sepals in the outer ring, for example, and sex organs in the innermost rings.

As is so often the case with complexity, the genes that build flowers are older than the flowers themselves. Gymnosperms turn out to carry flower-building genes even though they don't make flowers. Scientists have yet to determine what those genes do in gymnosperms, but their presence indicates that these genes probably existed in the common ancestor of gymnosperms and flowering plants.

In the flowering plant lineage those genes were borrowed to map out the structure of the flower. The first flowers were simple. But over time, the genes were duplicated accidentally, freeing one copy to take on a new role in flower development. Flowers grew more complex, and some of their parts gained new functions, such as luring insects with bright colors and fragrance.

This flexibility may help explain the success of flowering plants. Some 250,000 known species of flowering plants exist today. Gymnosperms, their flowerless relatives, are stuck at just over 800.

Complexity in Miniature

Some of life's most marvelous structures are its smallest: the minute clockwork of molecules that make cells tick. *E. coli,* a bacterium found in the gut, swims with a tiny spinning tail made up of several dozen different proteins, all working together. Doubters of evolution are fond of pointing out that the flagellum, as this tail is called, needs every one of its parts to function. They argue that it could not have evolved bit by bit; it must have been created in its present form.

But by comparing the flagellar proteins to those in other bacterial structures, Mark Pallen of the University of Birmingham in England and his colleagues have found clues to how this intricate mechanism was assembled from simpler parts. For example, *E. coli* builds its flagellum with a kind of pump that squirts out proteins. The pump is nearly identical, protein for protein, to another pump found on many disease-causing bacteria, which use it not for building a tail but for priming a molecular syringe that injects toxins into host cells. The similarity is, in Pallen's words, "an echo of history, because they have a common ancestor."

Scientists have discovered enough of these echoes to envision how *E. coli*'s flagellum could have evolved. Pallen proposes that its pieces—all of which have counterparts in today's microbes—came together step-by-step over millions of years. It all started with a pump-and-syringe assembly like those found on pathogens. In time, the syringe acquired a long needle, then a flexible hook at its base. Eventually it was linked to a power source: another kind of pump found in the cell membranes of many bacteria. Once the structure had a motor that could make it spin, the needle turned into a propeller, and microbes had new mobility.

Whether or not that's the full story, there is plenty of other evidence that natural selection has been at work on the flagellum. Biologists have identified scores of different kinds of flagella in various strains of bacteria. Some are thick and some are thin; some are mounted on the end of the cell and some on the side; some are powered by sodium ions and some by hydrogen ions. It's just the kind of variation that natural selection is expected to produce as it tailors a structure to the needs of different organisms.

Darwin also argued that complex features can decay over time. Ostriches are descended from flying birds, for example, but their wings became useless as they evolved into full-time runners. It turns out that microbial tails can become vestigial as well. Although *E. coli* is believed to make only one kind of tail, it also carries the remnants of genes for a second type. "You expect to see the baggage of history," says Pallen.

Evolution, ruthless and practical, is equally capable of building the most wonderful structures and tossing them aside when they're no longer needed.

Wonderful Life See more of evolution's intricate designs in a photo gallery, explore related links, and join a forum on human origins at **ngm.com/0611.**

15 Answers to Creationist Nonsense

Opponents of Evolution Want to Make a Place for Creationism by Tearing Down Real Science, But Their Arguments Don't Hold Up

By John Rennie

When Charles Darwin introduced the theory of evolution through natural selection 143 years ago, the scientists of the day argued over it fiercely, but the massing evidence from paleontology, genetics, zoology, molecular biology and other fields gradually established evolution's truth beyond reasonable doubt. Today that battle has been won everywhere—except in the public imagination.

Embarrassingly, in the 21st century, in the most scientifically advanced nation the world has ever known, creationists can still persuade politicians, judges and ordinary citizens that evolution is a flawed poorly supported fantasy. They lobby for creationist ideas such as "intelligent design" to be taught as alternatives to evolution in science classrooms. As this article goes to press, the Ohio Board of Education is debating whether to mandate such a change. Some antievolutionists such as Philip E. Johnson, a law professor at the University of California at Berkeley and author of *Darwin on Trial,* admit that they intend for intelligent design theory to serve as a "wedge" for reopening science classrooms to discussions of God.

Besieged teachers and others may increasingly find themselves on the spot to defend evolution and refute creationism. The arguments that creationists use are typically specious and based on misunderstandings of (or outright lies about) evolution, but the number and diversity of the objections can put even well-informed people at a disadvantage.

To help with answering them, the following list rebuts some of the most common "scientific" arguments raised against evolution. It also directs readers to further sources for information and explains why creation science has no place in the classroom.

1. Evolution is only a theory. It is not a fact or a scientific law.

Many people learned in elementary school that a theory falls in the middle of a hierarchy of certainty—above a mere hypothesis but below a law. Scientists do not use the terms that way, however. According to the National Academy of Sciences (**NAS**), a scientific theory is "a well-substantiated explanation of some aspect of the natural world that can incorporate facts laws, inferences, and tested hypotheses." No amount of validation changes a theory into a law which is a descriptive generalization about nature. So when scientists talk about the theory of evolution—or the atomic theory or the theory of relativity for that matter—they are not expressing reservations about its truth.

In addition to the *theory* of evolution meaning the idea of descent with modification, one may also speak of *the fact* of evolution. The **NAS** defines a fact as "an observation that has been repeatedly confirmed and for all practical purposes is accepted as "true". The fossil record and abundant other evidence testify that organisms have evolved through time. Although no one observed those transformations,

John Rennie, "15 Answers to Creationist Nonsense," from *Scientific American*; July 2002, pp. 78-85. Published by Scientific American, Inc., 2002. Copyright by Nature Publishing Group. Permission to reprint granted by the rights holder.

the indirect evidence is clear unambiguous and compelling.

All sciences frequently rely on indirect evidence. Physicists cannot see subatomic panicles directly for instance, so they verify their existence by watching for tell-tale tracks that the particles leave in cloud chambers. The absence of direct observation does not make physicists' conclusions less certain.

2. Natural selection is based on circular reasoning: The fittest are those who survive, and those who survive are deemed fittest.

"Survival of the fittest" is a conversational way to describe natural selection but a more technical description speaks of differential rates of survival and reproduction. This is, rather than labeling species as more or less fit, one can describe how many offspring they are likely to leave under given circumstances. Drop a fast-breeding pair of small-beaked finches and a slower-breeding pair of large-beaked finches onto an island full of food seeds. Within a few generations the fast breeders may control more of the food resources. Yet if large beaks more easily crush seeds, the advantage may tip to the slow breeders. In a pioneering study of finches on the Galapagos Islands, Peter R. Grant of Princeton University observed these kinds of population shifts in the wild see his article "Natural Selection and Darwin's Finches", *Scientific American,* October 1991

The key is that adaptive fitness can be defined without reference to survival: large beaks are better adapted for crushing seeds, irrespective of whether that trait has survival value under the circumstances.

3, Evolution is unscientific, because it is not testable or falsifiable. It makes claims about events that were not observed and can never be re-created.

This blanket dismissal of evolution ignores important distinctions that divide the field into at least two broad areas: microevolution and macroevolution. Microevolution looks at changes within species over time—changes that may be preludes to speciation, the origin of new species. Macroevolution studies how taxonomic groups above the level of species change. Its evidence draws frequently from the fossil record and DNA comparisons to reconstruct how various organisms may be related.

These days even most creationists acknowledge that microevolution has been upheld by tests in the laboratory (as in studies of cells, plants and fruit flies) and in the field (as in Grant's studies of evolving beak shapes among Galapagos finches). Natural selection and other mechanisms—such as chromosomal changes, symbiosis and hybridization—can drive profound changes in populations over time.

The historical nature of macroevolutionary study involves inference from fossils and DNA rather than direct observation. Yet in the historical sciences (which include astronomy, geology and archaeology as well as evolutionary biology), hypotheses can still be tested by checking whether they accord with physical evidence and whether they lead to verifiable predictions about future discoveries. For instance evolution implies that between the earliest-known ancestors of humans (roughly five million years old) and the appearance of anatomically modem humans (about 100,000 years ago), one should find a succession of hominid creatures with features progressively less apelike and more modem, which is indeed what the fossil record shows. But one should not—and does not—find modern human fossils embedded in strata from the Jurassic period (65 million years ago). Evolutionary biology routinely makes predictions far more refined and precise than this and researchers test them constantly.

Evolution could be disproved in other ways, too. If we could document the spontaneous generation of just one complex life-form from inanimate matter, then at least a few creatures seen in the fossil record might have originated this way. If superintelligent aliens appeared and claimed credit for creating life on earth (or even particular species), the purely evolutionary explanation would be cast in doubt. But no one has yet produced such evidence.

It should be noted that the idea of falsifiability as the defining characteristic of science originated with philosopher Karl Popper in the 1930s. More recent elaborations on his thinking have expanded the narrowest interpretation of his principle precisely because it would eliminate too many branches of clearly scientific endeavor.

Galapagos finches show adaptive beak shapes.

4. Increasingly, scientists doubt the truth of evolution.

No evidence suggests that evolution is losing adherents. Pick up any issue of a peer-reviewed biological journal, and you will find articles that support and extend evolutionary studies or that embrace evolution as a fundamental concept

Conversely, serious scientific publications disputing evolution are all but nonexistent. In the mid-1990s George W. Gilchrist of the University of Washington surveyed thousands of journals in the primary literature, seeking articles on intelligent design or creation science. Among those hundreds of thousands of scientific reports, he found none. In the past two years, surveys done independently by Barbara Forrest of Southeastern Louisiana University and Lawrence M. Krauss of Case Western Reserve University have been similarly fruitless.

Creationists retort that a closed-minded scientific community rejects their evidence. Yet according to the editors of *Nature*, *Science* and other leading journals, few antievolution manuscripts are even submitted. Some antievolution authors have published papers in serious journals. Those papers, however rarely attack evolution directly or advance creationist arguments: at best, they identify certain evolutionary problems as unsolved and difficult (which no one disputes). In short, creationists are not giving the scientific world good reason to take them seriously.

5. The disagreements among even evolutionary biologists show how little solid science supports evolution.

Evolutionary biologists passionately debate diverse topics: how speciation happens, the rates of evolutionary change the ancestral relationships of birds and dinosaurs, whether Neandertals were a species apart from modem humans and much more. These disputes are like those found in all other branches of science. Acceptance of evolution as a factual occurrence and a guiding principle is nonetheless universal in biology.

Unfortunately, dishonest creationists have shown a willingness to take scientists' comments out of context to exaggerate and distort the disagreements. Anyone acquainted with the works of paleontologist Stephen Jay Gould of Harvard University knows that in addition to co-authoring the punctuated equilibrium model, Gould was one of the most eloquent defenders and articulators of evolution. (Punctuated equilibrium explains patterns in the fossil record by suggesting that most evolutionary changes occur within geologically brief intervals—which may nonetheless amount to hundreds of generations.) Yet creationists delight in dissecting out phrases from Gould's voluminous prose to make him sound as though he had doubted evolution, and they present punctuated equilibrium as though it allows new species to materialize overnight or birds to be born from reptile eggs.

When confronted with a quotation from a scientific authority that seems to question evolution, insist on seeing the statement in context. Almost invariably, the attack on evolution will prove illusory.

6. If humans descended from monkeys, why are there still monkeys?

This surprisingly common argument reflects several levels of ignorance about evolution. The first mistake is that evolution does not teach that humans descended from monkeys; it states that both have a common ancestor.

The deeper error is that this objection is tantamount to asking, "If children descended from adults, why are there still adults?" New species evolve by splintering off from established ones, when populations of organisms become isolated from the main branch of their family and acquire sufficient differences to remain forever distinct. The parent species may survive indefinitely thereafter, or it may become extinct.

7. Evolution cannot explain how life first appeared on earth.

The origin of life remains very much a mystery, but biochemists have learned about how primitive nucleic acids, amino acids and other building blocks of life could have formed and organized themselves into self-replicating, self-sustaining units, laying the foundation for cellular biochemistry. Astrochemical analyses hint that quantities of these compounds might have originated in space and fallen to earth in comets, a scenario that may solve the problem of how those constituents arose under the conditions that prevailed when our planet was young.

Creationists sometimes try to invalidate all of evolution by pointing to science's current inability to explain the origin of life But even if life on earth turned out to have a non-evolutionary origin (for instance, if aliens introduced the first cell billions of years ago), evolution since then would be robustly confirmed by countless microevolutionary and macroevolutionary studies.

8. Mathematically, it is inconceivable that anything as complex as a protein, let alone a living cell or a human, could spring up by chance.

Chance plays a part in evolution (for example, in the random mutations that can give rise to new traits), but evolution does not depend on chance to create organisms, proteins or other entities. Quite the opposite: natural selection, the principal known mechanism of evolution, harnesses nonrandom change by preserving "desirable" (adaptive) features and eliminating "undesirable" (non-adaptive) ones. As long as the forces of selection stay constant, natural selection can push evolution in one direction and produce sophisticated structures in surprisingly short times.

As an analogy, consider the 13-letter sequence TOBEORNOTTOBE." Those hypothetical million monkeys, each pecking out one phrase a second,

could take as long as 78,800 years to find it among the 26^{13} sequences of that length. But in the 1980s Richard Hardison of Glendale College wrote a computer program that generated phrases randomly while preserving the positions of individual letters that happened to be correctly placed (in effect, selecting for phrases more like Hamlet's). On average, the program re-created the phrase in just 336 iterations, less than 90 seconds. Even more amazing, it could reconstruct Shakespeare's entire play in just four and a half days.

9. The Second Law of Thermodynamics says that systems must become more disordered over time. Living cells therefore could not have evolved from inanimate chemicals, and multicellular life could not have evolved from protozoa.

This argument derives from a misunderstanding of the Second Law. If it were valid, mineral crystals and snowflakes would also be impossible, because they are complex structures that form spontaneously from disordered parts.

The Second Law actually states that the total entropy of a closed system (one that no energy that matter leaves or enters) cannot decrease. Entropy is a physical concept often casually described as disorder, but it differs significantly from the conversational use of the word.

"God Created Humans in Their Present Form Within the Past 10,000 Years or So."

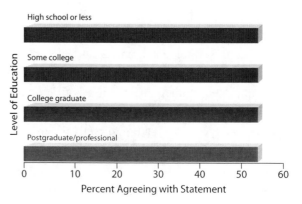

Cleo Vilett
Source: The Gallup Organization, 1999.

More important, however, the Second Law permits parts of a system to decrease in entropy as long as other parts experience an offsetting increase. Thus, our planet as a whole can grow more complex because the sun pours heat and light onto it, and the greater entropy associated with the sun's nuclear fusion more than rebalances the-scales. Simple organisms can fuel their rise toward complexity by consuming other forms of life and nonliving materials.

10. Mutations are essential to evolution theory, but mutation can only eliminate traits. They cannot produce new features.

On the contrary, biology has catalogued many traits produced point mutations (changes at precise positions in an organism DNA)—bacterial resistance to antibiotics, for example.

Mutations that arise in the homeobox (*Hox*) family of development-regulating genes in animals can also have complex effects. Hex genes direct where legs, wings, antennae and body segments should grow. In fruit flies, for instance, the mutation called *Antennapedia* causes legs to sprout where antennae should grow. These abnormal limbs are not functional, but their existence demonstrates that genetic mistakes can produce complex structures, which natural selection can then test for possible uses.

Moreover, molecular biology has discovered mechanisms for genetic change that go beyond point mutations, and these expand the ways in which new traits can appear. Functional modules within genes can be spliced together in novel ways. Whole genes can he accidentally duplicated in an organism's DNA. and the duplicates are free to mutate into genes for new, complex features. Comparisons of the DNA from a wide variety of organisms indicate that this is how the globin family of blood proteins evolved over millions of years

11. Natural selection might explain microevolution, but it cannot explain the origin of new species and higher orders of life,

Evolutionary biologists have written extensively about how natural selection could produce new species. For instance, in the model called allopatry, developed by Ernst Mayr of Harvard University, if in population of organisms were isolated from the rest of its species by geographical boundaries, it might be subjected to different selective pressures. Changes would accumulate in the isolated population. If those changes became so significant that the splinter group could not or routinely would not breed with the original stock, then the ter group would be *reproductively isolated* and on its way toward becoming a new species.

Natural selection is the best studied of the evolutionary mechanisms, but biologists are open to other possibilities as well. Biologists are constantly assessing the potential of unusual genetic mechanism for causing speciation or for producing complex features in organisms. Lynn Margulis of the University of Massachusetts at Amherst and others have persuasively argued that some cellular organelles such as the energy-generating mitochondria, evolved through the symbiotic merger of ancient organisms. Thus, science welcomes the possibility of evolution resulting from forces beyond natural selection. Yet those forces must be natural; they cannot be attributed to the actions of mysterious creative intelligences whose existence, in scientific terms, is unproved.

12. Nobody has ever seen a new species evolve.

Speciation is probably fairly rare and in many cases might take centuries. Furthermore, recognizing a new species during a formative stage can be difficult, because biologists sometimes disagree about how best to define a species. The most widely used definition, Mayr's Biological Species Concept, recognizes a species as a distinct community of reproductively isolated populations—sets of organisms that normally do not or cannot breed outside their community. In practice, this standard can be difficult to apply to organisms isolated by distance or terrain or to plants (and, of course, fossils do not breed). Biologists therefore usually use organisms' physical and behavioral traits as clues to their species membership.

Nevertheless, the scientific literature does contain reports of apparent speciation events in plants, insects and worms. In most of these experiments, researchers subjected organisms to various types of selection—for anatomical differences, mating behaviors, habitat preferences and other traits—and found that they had created populations of organisms that did not breed with outsiders. For example, William R. Rice of the University of New Mexico and George W. Salt of the University of California at Davis demonstrated that if they sorted a group of fruit flies by their preference for certain environments and bred those flies separately over 35 generations, the resulting flies would refuse to breed with those from a very different environment.

13. Evolutionists cannot point to any transitional fossils—creatures that are half reptile and half bird, for instance.

Actually, paleontologists know of many detailed examples of fossils intermediate in form between various taxonomic groups. One of the most famous fossils of all time is *Archaeopteryx*, which combines feathers and skeletal structures peculiar to birds with features of dinosaurs. A flock's worth of other feathered fossil species, some more avian and some less, has also been found. A sequence of fossils spans the evolution of modern horses from the tiny *Eohippus*. Whales had four-legged ancestors that walked on land, and creatures known as *Ambulocetus* and *Rodhocetus* helped to make that transition (see "The Mammals That Conquered the Seas," by Kate Wong; *Scientific American,* May). Fossil seashells trace the evolution of various mollusks through millions of years. Perhaps 20 or more hominids (not all of them our ancestors) fill the gap between Lucy the australopithecine and modern humans.

Creationists, though, dismiss these fossil studies. They argue that *Archaeopteryx* is not a missing link between reptiles and birds—it is just an extinct bird with reptilian features. They want evolutionists to produce a weird, chimeric monster that cannot be classified as belonging to any known group. Even if a creationist does accept a fossil as transitional between two species, he or she may then insist on seeing other fossils intermediate between it and the first two. These frustrating requests can proceed ad infinitum and place an unreasonable burden on the always incomplete fossil record

Nevertheless, evolutionists can cite further supportive evidence from molecular biology. All organisms share most of the same genes, but as evolution predicts, the structures of these genes and their products diverge among species, in keeping with their evolutionary relationships. Geneticists speak of the "molecular clock" that records the passage of time. These molecular data also show how various organisms are transitional within evolution.

14. Living things have fantastically intricate features—at the anatomical, cellular and molecular levels—that could not function If they were any less complex or sophisticated. The only prudent conclusion is that they are the products of intelligent design, not evolution.

This "argument from design" is the backbone of most recent attacks on evolution, but it is also one of the oldest. In 1802 theologian William Paley wrote that if one finds a pocket watch in a field, the most reasonable conclusion is that someone dropped it, not that natural forces created it there. By analogy Paley argued, the complex structures of living things must be the handiwork of direct divine invention. Darwin wrote *On the Origin of Species* as an answer to Paley he explained bow natural forces of selection, acting on inherited features, could gradually shape the evolution of ornate organic structures.

Generations of creationists have tried to counter Darwin by citing the example of the eye as a structure that could not have evolved. The eye's ability to provide vision depends on the perfect arrangement of its parts these critics say. Natural selection could thus never favor the transitional forms needed during the eye's evolution—what good is half an eye? Anticipating this criticism, Darwin suggested that even "incomplete" eyes might confer benefits (such as helping creatures orient toward light) and thereby survive for further evolutionary refinement Biology has vindicated Darwin: researchers have identified primitive eyes and light-sensing organs throughout the animal kingdom and have even tracked the evolutionary history of eyes through comparative genetics. (It now appears that in various families of organisms, eyes have evolved independently.)

Today's intelligent-design advocates are more sophisticated than their predecessors, but their arguments and goals are not fundamentally different. They criticize evolution by trying to that it could nor account for life as we know it and then insist that the only tenable alternative is that life was designed by an unidentified intelligence.

15. Recent discoveries prove that even at the microscopic level, life has a quality of complexity that could not have come about through evolution.

"Irreducible complexity" is the battle cry of Michael J. Behe of Lehigh University, author of *Darwin's Black Box: The Biochemical Challenge to Evolution.* As a household example, of irreducible complexity, Behe chooses the mousetrap—a machine that could not function if any of its pieces were missing and whose pieces have no value except as parts of the whole. What is true of the mousetrap, he says, is even truer of the bacterial flagellum, a whip like cellular organelle used for propulsion that operates like an outboard motor. The proteins that make up a flagellum are uncannily arranged into motor components, a universal joint and other structures like those that a human engineer might specify. The possibility that this intricate array could have arisen through evolutionary modification is virtually nil, Behe argues, and that bespeaks intelligent design. He makes similar points about the blood's clotting mechanism and other molecular systems.

Yet evolutionary biologists have answers to these objections. First there exist flagellae with forms simpler than the one that Behe cites, so it is not necessary for all those components to be present for a flagellum to work. The sophisticated components of this flagellum all have precedents elsewhere in nature, as described by Kenneth R. Miller of Brown University and others. In fact, the entire flagellum assembly is extremely similar to an organelle that *Yersinia pestis,* the bubonic plague bacterium, uses to inject toxins into cells.

The key is that the flagellum's component structures, which Behe suggests have no value apart from their role in propulsion, can serve multiple functions that would have helped favor their evolution. The final evolution of the flagellum might then have involved only the novel recombination of sophisticated parts that initially evolved for other purposes. Similarly, the blood-cloning system seems to involve the modification and elaboration of proteins that were originally used in digestion, according to studies by Russell F. Doolittle of the University of California at San Diego. So some of the complexity that Behe calls proof of intelligent design is not irreducible at all.

Complexity of a different kind—"specified complexity"—is the cornerstone of the intelligent-design arguments of William A. Dembeski of Baylor University in his books **The Design Inference** and **No free Lunch.** Essentially his argument is that living things are complex in a way that undirected, random processes could never produce. The only logical conclusion, Dembski asserts, in an echo of Paley 200 years ago, is that some superhuman intelligence created and shaped life.

Dembski's argument contains several holes. It is wrong to insinuate that the field of explanations consists only of random processes or designing intelligences. Researchers into nonlinear systems and cellular automata at the Santa Fe Institute and elsewhere have demonstrated that simple, undirected processes can yield extraordinarily complex patterns. Some of the complexity seen in organisms therefore emerge through natural phenomena that

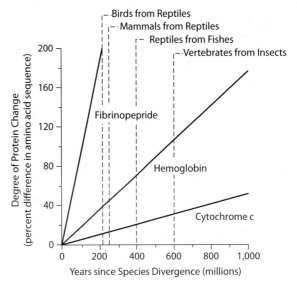

PROTEIN EVOLUTION REFLECTS SPECIES DIVERGENCE

Cleo Vilett

we as yet barely understand. But that is far different from saying that the complexity could not have arisen naturally.

"Creation science" is a contradiction in terms. A central tenet of modern science is methodological naturalism it seeks to explain the universe purely in terms of observed or testable natural mechanisms. Thus, physics describes the atomic nucleus with specific concepts governing matter and energy, and it tests those descriptions experimentally. Physicists introduce new particles, such as quarks, to flesh out their theories only when data show that the previous descriptions cannot adequately explain observed phenomena. The new particles do not have arbitrary properties, moreover—their definitions are tightly constrained, because the new particles must fit within the existing framework of physics.

In contrast, intelligent-design theorists invoke shadowy entities that conveniently have whatever unconstrained abilities are needed to solve the mystery at hand. Rather than expanding scientific inquiry, such answers shut it down. (How does one disprove the existence of omnipotent intelligences?)

Intelligent design offers few answers. For instance, when and how did a designing intelligence intervene in fife's history? By creating the first DNA? The first cell? The first human? Was every species designed, or just a few early ones? Proponents of intelligent-design theory frequently decline to be pinned down on these points. They do not even make real attempts to reconcile their disparate ideas about intelligent design. Instead they pursue argument by exclusion—that is, they belittle evolutionary explanations as far-fetched or incomplete and then imply that only design-based alternatives remain.

Logically, this is misleading: even if one naturalistic explanation is flawed, it does not mean that all are. Moreover, it does not make one intelligent-design theory more reasonable than another. Listeners are essentially left to fill in the blanks for themselves, and some will undoubtedly do so by substituting their religious beliefs for scientific ideas.

Time and again, science has shown that methodological naturalism can push back ignorance, finding increasingly detailed and informative answers to mysteries that once seemed impenetrable: the nature of light. the causes of disease, how the brain works. Evolution is doing the same with the riddle of how the living world took shepe. Creationism, by any name, adds nothing of intellectual value to the effort.

JOHN RENNIE is editor in chief of *Scientific American.*

From *Scientific American,* July 2002. pp. 78-85. Copyright © 2002 by Scientific American. Reprinted by permission. References and notes omitted

Other Resources for Defending Evolution

How to Debate a Creationist: 25 Creationists' Arguments and 25 Evolutionists' Answers. Michael Shermer. Skeptics Society, 1997. This well-researched refutation of creationist claims deals in more depth with many of the same scientific arguments raised here, as well as other philosophical problems. *Skeptic* magazine routinely covers creation/evolution debates and is a solid, thoughtful source on the subject. **www.skeptic.com**

Defending Evolution In the Classroom: A Guide to the Creation/Evolution Controversy. Brian J. Afters and Sandra M. Afters. Jones and Bartlett Publishers, 2001. This up-to-date overview of the creation/evolution controversy explores the issues clearly and readably, with a full appreciation of the cultural and religious influences that create resistance to teaching evolution. It, too, uses a question and-answer format that should be particularly valuable for teachers.

Science and Creationism: A View from the National Academy of Sciences. Second edition. National Academy Press, 1999 This concise booklet has the backing of the country's top scientific authorities. Although its goal of making a dear, brief statement necessarily limits the detail with which it can pursue its arguments, the publication serves as handy proof that the scientific establishment unwaveringly supports evolution. It is also available at **www.nationalacademies.org/evolution/**

The Triumph of Evolution and the Failure of Creationism. Niles Eldredge. W. H. Freeman and Company, 2000. The author, a leading contributor to evolution theory and a curator at the American Museum of Natural History in New York City, offers a scathing critique of evolution's opponents.

Intelligent Design Creationism and Its Critics. Edited by Robert T. Pennock. Bradford Books/MIT Press, 2001. For anyone who wishes to understand the "intelligent design" controversy in detail, this book is a terrific one-volume summary of the scientific philosophical and theological issues. Philip E. Johnson, Michael J. Behe and William A. Dembski make the case for intelligent design in their chapters and are rebutted by evolutionists, including Pennock, Stephen Jay Gould and Richard Dawkins.

Talk Origins archive (www.talkorigins.org) This wonderfully thorough online resource compiles useful essays and commentaries that have appeared in usenet discussions about creationism and evolution. It offers detailed discussions (some of which may be too sophisticated for casual readers) and bibliographies relating to virtually any objection to evolution that creationists might raise.

National Center for Science Education Web site (www. ncseweb.org). The center is the only national organization that specializes in defending the teaching of evolution against creationist attacks. Offering resources for combating misinformation and monitoring antievolution legislation, it is ideal for staying current with the ongoing public debate.

PBS Web site for evolution (www.pbs.org/wgbh/ evolution/). Produced as a companion to the seven-part television series *Evolution,* this site is an enjoyable guide to evolutionary science. It features multimedia tools for teaching evolution. The accompanying book, *Evolution,* by Carl Zimmer (HarperCollins, 2001), is also useful for explaining evolution to doubters.

Portrait in DNA

Can Forensic Analysis Yield Police-Style Sketches of Suspects?

By Christine Soares

Male, short and stout, with dark skin, brown eyes, shovel-shaped teeth, type A+ blood and coarse, dark brown hair giving way to pattern baldness. He would have a high tolerance for alcohol and a higher-than-average risk of nicotine dependence—fortunately, he lived thousands of years before humans discovered smoking. The description of a Stone Age Greenland resident published in February paints an extraordinary portrait of a man who vanished more than 4,000 years ago, drawn almost solely from his DNA remains.

The analysis, led by Danish scientists, not only marks the first full sequencing of an ancient human genome but also offers a startling example of how much modern-day detectives can discern just from a suspect's genetic code. Far beyond using DNA "fingerprints" to link an individual to a crime scene, forensic profiling is edging toward the capability to create a police-artist-style sketch of an unknown person by reading traits inscribed in the genome. "The body interprets the DNA to determine the appearance of the face," says anthropologist Mark Shriver of Morehouse College, who hopes to duplicate that ability within a decade.

The scientists reconstructing the ancient Greenlander had only a few tufts of hair, preserved in permafrost, from which they extracted DNA. The hair itself is dark and thick and contains chemical traces indicating mainly a seafood diet. From the man's genes, the researchers resolved a long-standing debate about the origins of Greenland's paleo-Eskimos by showing he had a pattern of DNA variations most common in Siberian population groups. Having established his ancestral origins in northern Asia, the team could then interpret variations called single-nucleotide polymorphisms (SNPs) in four genes linked to brown eye color in modern Asians. The same method revealed SNPs associated with shovel-shaped front teeth and a dry type of ear-wax, both traits common in modern Asians and Native Americans. Four more SNPs suggest that he probably had dark skin. Another set of variations typical of populations adapted to cold climates indicates he had a compact body and ample body fat.

Together those traits might not make the ancient Greenlander stand out in a lineup, but they could dramatically narrow the search for suspects. A handful of high-profile criminal cases has already demonstrated the utility of even basic prospective information. In 2007 Christopher Phillips and his colleagues at the University of Santiago de Compostela in Spain used markers in a DNA sample obtained from a toothbrush to identify a suspect in the 2004 Madrid train bombing as being of North African descent. Police later confirmed that the terrorist was Algerian. In an infamous Louisiana serial killer investigation, witness testimony had indicated a Caucasian culprit, but DNA evidence pointed to someone of significant African-American and

Native American descent. Police widened their search and eventually caught the killer.

Having more to go on than ancestry, a generally poor indicator of appearance, is the goal of programs such as the DNA Initiative of the National Institute of Justice, which funds research into alternative genetic markers for forensic use. Daniele Podini of George Washington University is developing a forensic kit to determine, by analyzing 50 to 100 genetic markers, a suspect's eye and hair color, sex and probable ancestry. "The idea is just to provide another investigational tool," he says, "one that can help corroborate the testimony of a witness or reduce the number of suspects."

Getting more specific gets significantly more difficult, Podini adds. DNA alone offers few clues to age, for instance. With whole cells, researchers could examine telomeres, the chromosomal end caps that wear away with time, but individual health and other factors can influence their shrinkage. One recent study showed that dedicated athletes in their 50s might have the telomeres of a 25-year-old. Another important feature in profiling, height, has hereditary roots but also depends on environmental factors, such as nutrition during childhood.

Nevertheless, pinning down the effects of genes that influence body development is the key to predicting a specific individual's looks. Shriver is studying populations in Europe and mixed-race groups elsewhere in the hope that correlating a Gallic nose or smiling Irish eyes with genes that influence their distinctive shapes may begin to crack the code the body uses to build a specific feature. He is even exposing inch-square patches of volunteers' skin to ultraviolet light to gauge the range of skin shades and tones possible for people with various racial and ethnic backgrounds.

Skin-deep is as far as a DNA sketch should go, according to some bioethicists. The ancient Greenlander also had an elevated risk for hypertension and diabetes. A modern all-points bulletin could, in principle, describe a suspect's pigmentation, ancestry, and higher-than-average likelihood of being obese, a smoker, alcoholic or just depressed. "I think there are some valid ethical issues around this kind of work," Shriver remarks.

Practical considerations may be what delays deployment of any but the simplest forensic kits, though. "The forensic field is very, very conservative," Podini says, "so before you actually apply something to casework, it has to be proven beyond a reasonable doubt as something that works well, is reliable and is accepted by the scientific community."

Chapter 2

Osteology

Enrollment in Human Osteology classes have increased over the last 10 years. This is due to the popularity of TV shows like *CSI* and *Bones*. Hence, there is great interest among undergraduate students in becoming a forensic anthropologist. The path to becoming a forensic anthropologist is a long one—you end up with a PhD in the field before you are qualified to work on a case. The need is great: As of 2008, there are only 103 forensic anthropologists in the United States. The "Introduction to Physical Anthropology" lab section is the first step toward this career goal. Students should be aware that skeletal biology is a subfield of human variation. The task of all students is to first learn the name of the bones (all 206 of them), and then identify them. During this process, we learn what is normal about human skeletal remains, and that what is normal comes across with considerable variation in their expression. Once what is normal is determined, then we can begin to understand and look for what is abnormal, or unexpected (skeletal lesions associated with health issues, fractured bones as the result of violent encounters, and bone oddities related to genetic disorders). In doing so, students learn about the subfield of paleopathology. Some of the articles in this reader explain this discipline in more detail.

Human osteology is not just about forensic work: It is also a key component to human evolution studies as well, since the fossil record is a reflection of skeletal anatomy from extinct and past species. What can be learned from the fossil record must start with understanding that skeletal features reflect a form-and-function relationship. Through the lens of biomechanical studies, anthropologists can begin to understand how extinct animals may have utilized their environment by how they walked, what they ate, and even how they may have socialized. To infer how form and function provides the findings offered by anthropologists, we often use cross-species comparisons. That is, we use nonhuman primate models (gorillas, chimps, and monkeys) in these comparisons. In doing so, it is necessary to have a good understanding of animal skeletal anatomy as well.

Reading the Bones of La Florida

By Clark Spencer Larsen

New approaches are offering insight into the lives of Native Americans after the Europeans arrived. Their health declined not only because of disease but because of their altered diet and living circumstances.

The lives of Native Americans changed in dramatic ways after Christopher Columbus landed in the Caribbean islands in 1492. Written records paint a vivid picture of conquest and epidemics sowing death and disease among the indigenous peoples of the Americas, quickly decimating them. Until recently, in fact, almost all that was known about the biological consequences of contact with the Europeans was based on these old documents, which emphasize epidemics and population collapse. Although these texts offer an important perspective, they are not the only source of information.

Bioarchaeology, an emerging field that focuses on the study of archaeological remains, is supplementing our view of the health and daily life of Native Americans, particularly those who lived in the Spanish missions of the Southeast, in an area once known as *La Florida*. Sustained encounters between Indians and Europeans in *La Florida* began in 1565, when Pedro Menendez de Aviles established the town of St. Augustine on the Atlantic coast in northern Florida. From there Roman Catholic priests set up a chain of missions among the Timucua and Apalachee Indians of northern Florida and the Guale Indians of the Georgia coast. At some of those places—including Santa Catalina de Guale on St. Catherines Island, San Martin de Timucua and San Luis de Apalachee—archaeologists have uncovered the ruins of large churches that served the converts. As the nucleus of each community, the church carried out important religious functions for the living; for the dead, it provided a burial ground.

Skeletons found beneath the floor of these churches have provided scholars with a surprisingly complete record of the diet and work habits of the mission Indians. Bioarchaeology is beginning to fill in the details of the historical record, offering specifics about how food sources changed and raising unexpected questions about the merits of a purely agricultural way of life—at least for the Indians who inhabited *La Florida*.

Food, obviously, is fundamental to human well-being, as it provides nutrients for growth, development and other physiological processes. Before our research, the diets of *La Florida* Indians were reconstructed from two sources: accounts by priests and other Europeans, and food remains at archaeological sites. The written records are often contradictory. Some depict little farming at the time. Others, including those examined by Grant D. Jones of Davidson College, say that indigenous peoples relied heavily on agriculture, particularly on corn.

The archaeological record is inconclusive as well. Plant remains do not always survive well, and in coastal regions they are particularly vulnerable to the destructive effects of moisture and acidic soils. Nevertheless, analysis of such evidence by C. Margaret Scarry of the University of North Carolina at Chapel Hill and Donna Ruhl of the University of Florida has revealed that native peoples ate numerous plant species, both wild and domesticated, before and after the arrival of the Europeans. But their use of corn is unclear. Excavations have revealed some kernels and cobs from late prehistoric and contact-era sites; however, the relative importance of this grain in the Indians' diet is not known.

Reconstructing Diet

To resolve some of these questions, we turned to the many bones found at these sites. Because the tissues of all living things contain stable isotopes of such elements as carbon and nitrogen, we can measure the amounts of these elements in bones and then use this information to reconstruct ancient diets. Differences in the ratios of two carbon isotopes, carbon 12 and carbon 13, contain a record of which plants an individual ate. Most plants are divided into two types: carbon 3 plants break down a three-carbon molecule during photosynthesis; carbon 4 plants synthesize a four-carbon molecule. The distinctive chemical signature of the C_3 and C_4

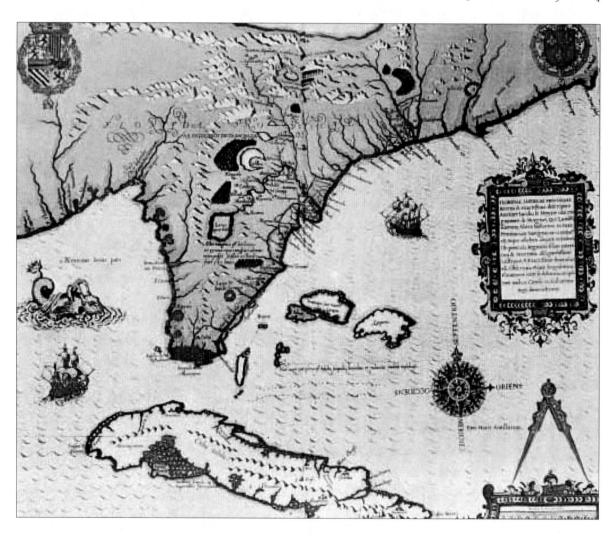

*LA FLORIDA **was viewed by the Spanish as fertile land for conquest, and the region's natives as souls to be converted and workers to be harnessed—particularly for the harvest of corn, which became increasingly important as a dietary staple** (far left).*

SPANISH MISSIONS, such as this one at San Luis de Apalachee (left), were established throughout what is now Florida and coastal Georgia. Serving three primary tribes—the Guale, the Apalachee and the Timucua—these missions became centers of social and religious life.

plants that a person consumes shows up in his or her bones. Virtually all plants eaten in the *La Florida* region were of the C_3 variety—including fruits, wheat, acorns and hickory nuts. The only major C_4 plant eaten by native peoples was corn.

Nitrogen isotopes provide a different set of clues. Fish bones and oyster shells in archaeological sites indicate that the Guale and other native peoples of the region ate seafood regularly—before and after the Europeans arrived. Because marine plants, such as algae, and terrestrial plants use the two stable isotopes of nitrogen—nitrogen 14 and nitrogen 15—differently, the ratios of these isotopes are different in the bones of a person who ate mostly marine foods as opposed to one who ate mostly terrestrial foods.

Examining the differences between carbon and nitrogen ratios in bones before and after the Europeans arrived pointed to enormous changes in the Native Americans' diets. Margaret J. Schoeninger of the University of Wisconsin-Madison, Nikolaas J. van der Merwe of Harvard University, Dale L. Hutchinson of East Carolina University, Lynette Norr of the University of Florida and I found that the variations were geographically and chronologically patterned. As would be expected, coastal people ate more seafood than inland people did, regardless of the era. The Guale Indians on St. Catherines and Amelia islands ate corn before

and after the missionaries arrived. But during the mission period, they ate more than their ancestors had. Similarly, the Apalachee, who had eaten some corn before contact, seemed to eat it more after the Europeans arrived; and the Timucua, who had eaten little or no corn before contact, also adopted it after the establishment of the missions.

The Consequences of Corn

The bone chemistry findings thus show that the Indians' diets changed after the Europeans came—but not for the better. Their relatively heterogeneous diet, rich in seafood and a variety of plants and animals, was replaced by a more homogeneous and less nutritious diet focused on the cultivation of a single crop: corn.

Corn-dominated diets are very poor ones. Corn contains a great deal of sugar, which promotes cavities and poor oral health in general. It also contains phytate, a chemical that binds with iron, inhibiting absorption of the mineral by the body. As a result, people whose diets are heavy in corn are predisposed to anemia and the many other consequences of low iron [see "Iron Deficiency," by Nevin S. Scrimshaw; SCIENTIFIC AMERICAN, October 1991]. To make matters worse for corn-dependent populations, growth and development are hampered because

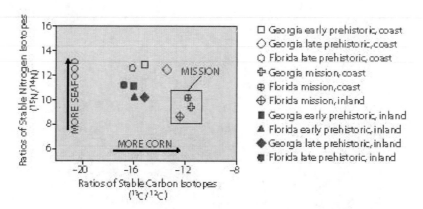

RATIOS OF ELEMENTS, such as carbon and nitrogen isotopes, provide important information about diet. Recorded in bones, these varying ratios reveal what kinds of plants or how much seafood an individual ate.

corn is a poor source of calcium and of niacin, or vitamin B_3, which is necessary for metabolism. Corn is also an inadequate source of protein because, depending on the strain, it is deficient in or entirely lacking three of the eight essential amino acids: lysine, isoleucine and tryptophan.

For these reasons, some mission Indians have more, and larger, cavities than their ancestors did. Tooth decay was probably exacerbated by the consistency of their food: soft foods, such as gruel made from corn, facilitate the buildup of cavity-causing bacteria and plaque on teeth. By looking at tooth wear with a scanning electron microscope, Mark F. Teaford and his colleagues at Johns Hopkins University have shown that the foods eaten by mission Indians were softer than those their ancestors ate. We can tell this by the reduction in the number of tooth-surface features, such as pits and scratches, caused by eating hard, non-agricultural food.

In places where diet varied, this general pattern shows some interesting departures. In collaboration with Bonnie G. McEwan of the Florida Bureau of Archaeological Research, we analyzed teeth from the San Luis mission site. Later work on the teeth by Tiffiny A. Tung of the University of North Carolina at Chapel Hill indicated that people in this mission had fewer cavities than did their counterparts at other sites. This departure from the usual pattern may have been explained by the research of Elizabeth J. Reitz of the University of Georgia, who examined animal remains at the same site. She determined that people living in San Luis had access

to beef—a rare addition to the mission Indians' standard diet—and that protein may have inhibited the formation of cavities.

The tooth record has provided us with other important insights as well. Hutchison and I have found that many Indians had hypoplasias—visible lines on teeth caused by disease or malnutrition. The large size of the hypoplasias in some Indians suggests that they experienced severe or sustained illness or poor nutrition, or both. We also found evidence of disturbances in tooth development. With Scott W. Simpson of Case Western Reserve University, we studied microscopic features of teeth, looking at what are called Retzius lines—growth lines that can be seen in enamel. Although both precontact and mission Indians have abnormal Retzius lines, these malformations are more prevalent in the mission Indians.

Considered together with other evidence, the increase in abnormal Retzius lines suggests that poor diet was not the only problem facing the mission Indians. David Hurst Thomas of the American Museum of Natural History in New York City has excavated a shallow, plank-lined well in Santa Catalina de Guale that may have served as a reservoir for parasites. Although their ancestors relied on freshwater streams and springs, the mission Indians drank well water, and anyone living in the region today knows the dangers of drinking water from shallow wells: it is easily contaminated and can cause parasitic infection and other problems.

The probability of rampant infection is strengthened by the fact that most of the defective tooth enamel we studied appears to have been formed during the first two years of life. This is a period when dehydration from infantile diarrhea is a primary health threat. Acute dehydration can inhibit the function of all forms of cells, including ameloblasts—the cells responsible for enamel formation. As in many underdeveloped nations today, bacteria and viruses in contaminated food and water cause infantile diarrhea. Certainly the mission would have created the kind of living circumstances that promote infantile diarrhea and the pattern of growth stress we have seen in teeth.

Other diseases, such as smallpox and measles, may have easily spread as well because the Indians were clustered together in crowded communities around the missions. Although many acute infectious diseases kill people long before their bones are affected, some infections—such as those caused by the bacterium *Staphylococcus aureus*—can travel from a soft-tissue wound to nearby bone, leaving observable lesions. Numerous lower-leg bones, or tibias, of contact-era Indians have lesions that suggest just this kind of infection.

Infection can also cause anemia because some types of parasite, such as hookworm, bleed their human hosts. Observations of mission bones indicate that such infection was common. The surfaces of many of these bones have sievelike lesions—called porotic hyperostosis—that can be caused by iron deficiency, scurvy or infection. Few precontact Indians seemed to have these lesions, probably because their diet of fish and maize together provided enough iron to stave off anemia. But the abundance of porotic hyperostosis in the mission Indians was most likely the result of the anemia brought on not simply by an increasingly corn-rich diet but also by intestinal infection.

Food and living conditions were not the only aspects of culture that were drastically altered for the Indians who lived in the missions. The Spanish practiced *repartimiento* draft labor in *La Florida,* which meant that able-bodied Indian men were required to work on farms, in public works and government building projects, and for the military. Indians were also required to carry heavy loads over long distances, because draft animals were not available

in the region until after 1680 or thereabouts. In our studies of skeletons, we noticed that contact-era Indians had a higher rate of osteoarthritis than their predecessors did—a phenomenon we believed had been caused by the increased workload, because wear and tear on the joints can lead to osteoarthritis. But the condition is related to other factors as well. So we decided to investigate further, looking to the skeletons for more answers.

Working Bones

The skeleton of a living person is highly responsive to physical activity. Throughout life a person's bones change shape and structure in response to mechanical forces acting on them. Basically, bone tissue is placed where the skeleton needs it. When a person walks, for example, or stands, forces deriving from the pull of muscles or from body weight trigger cellular activity in the bone that results in skeletal remodeling. Without the proper amount or distribution of bone in key places, the force of bending or twisting could break the thigh bone, or femur.

Drawing from methods developed by civil and mechanical engineers for measuring the strength of building materials, Christopher B. Ruff of the Johns Hopkins University School of Medicine and I have analyzed the strength of femur and humerus (upper-arm) bones from both precontact and mission sites in *La Florida.* This approach entails measuring cross-sectional geometric properties of the bones called second moments of area. Second moments of area reflect how the bone is distributed in cross section and indicate the strength or ability of the bone to resist breaking during bending or twisting. The analysis entails tracing the profile of the outer (subperiosteal) and inner (endosteal) perimeters of the bones in cross section and then calculating the biomechanical properties of the bone [see *illustration above*].

We discovered that the mission Indians had stronger bones than their predecessors did: the later bones had greater second moments of area than the earlier bones. This is not to say that the bones of the mission Indians were better than those of their ancestors. Rather the bones had just adapted to new mechanical demands. Given the well-known circumstance of exploitation and the heavy workloads of the Indians laboring under the Europeans, we believe that the increases in bone strength and osteoarthritis were caused by fundamental alterations in their way of life that involved increased physical activity.

The insights afforded us by bioarchaeology confirm much of what is found in historical texts—including the forced labor of the Indians and the diseases that plagued them—but they also give us a much more comprehensive and precise picture of the past. European contact introduced hardships for the Indians on many fronts. Pestilence, poor nutrition, iron deficiency, growth disruption, infection and hard labor all took their toll. Yet despite the unfavorable state of affairs, native peoples accommodated new demands and new challenges, a story that is repeated time and again in the history of our species.

The Author

CLARK SPENCER LARSEN directs the La Florida Bioarchaeology Project, which involves the collaboration of many scientists from the U.S. and abroad. He began his studies of ancient human skeletons in his freshman year at Kansas State University, where he received his B.A. in 1974. His doctorate in biological anthropology was awarded by the University of Michigan in 1980. Larsen is Ames Hawley Professor of Anthropology at the University of North Carolina at Chapel Hill and is a research associate with the American Museum of Natural History in New York City. Larsen is currently president of the American Association of Physical Anthropologists.

Further Information

THE ARCHAEOLOGY OF MISSION SANTA CATALINA DE GUALE, Vol. : SEARCH AND DISCOVERY. David Hurst Thomas. *Anthropological Papers of the American Museum of Natural History,* Vol. 63, Part 2, pages 47-161; June 12, 1987.

AGRICULTURE among the mission Indians, such as the Timucua depicted in this 16th-century engraving, increased enormously after the Spanish arrived. The shift was not beneficial for the natives of *La Florida.* **Agriculture ultimately forced them to simplify their diet to such a degree that their health suffered.**

THE ARCHAEOLOGY OF MISSION SANTA CATALINA DE GUALE, Vol. 2: BIOCULTURAL INTERPRETATIONS OF A POPULATION IN TRANSITION. Edited by Clark Spencer Larsen. *Anthropological Papers of the American Museum of Natural History,* No. 68; 1990.

IN THE WAKE OF CONFLICT: BIOLOGICAL RESPONSES TO CONQUEST. Edited by Clark Spencer Larsen and George R. Milner. Wiley-Liss, 1994.

THE APALACHEE INDIANS AND MISSION SAN LUIS. John H. Hahn and Bonnie G. McEwan. University Press of Florida, 1998.

REGIONAL VARIATION IN THE PATTERN OF MAIZE ADOPTION AND USE IN FLORIDA AND GEORGIA. Dale L. Hutchinson, Clark Spencer Larsen, Margaret J. Schoeninger and Lynette Norr in *American Antiquity,* Vol. 63, No. 3, pages 397-416; July 1998.

SKELETONS IN OUR CLOSET: REVEALING OUR PAST THROUGH BIOARCHAEOLOGY. Clark Spencer Larsen. Princeton University Press, 2000.

Where Are the Bodies?

In the Ground

By Richard Wright

Abstract: The subject of this essay is the judicial context of bodies from mass graves. I shall discuss topics that exemplify the power that flows from being able to display bodies to courts. By contrast, and where there are no bodies to show, a lazy prosecution case can be weakened by the unnecessary lack of material evidence. Particularly vulnerable are cases that depend on the statements of eye-witnesses. I shall discuss efforts by revisionists to protect their positions. These efforts include denying that there are any bodies as well as claims that the number of bodies is less than expected and that the bodies are attributable to unrelated events. These discussions will be illustrated with critical evidentiary photos.

Key words: Archaeology, mass graves, forensic, evidentiary, gruesome images in court.

"Where are the bodies?" is the question posed by the title of this special issue of *The Public Historian*. In an overwhelming number of cases, the answer is "In the ground." Because the bodies are in the ground, they are in archaeological territory. So it is up to archaeologists to find and recover the bodies and associated artifacts. That has been my job, on and off, since 1990—the job of a forensic archaeologist. Forensic archaeology has two purposes—the evidentiary and the humanitarian. The evidentiary work is for courts and the humanitarian work is for relatives and friends of the dead.

My forensic archaeological work has been evidentiary, that is, done at the request of prosecutors and intended for courts. So my teams and I have been finding graves by examining the surface of the ground, digging down and exposing the bodies, recording associated evidence, and then exhuming the bodies and sending them off to a mortuary for postmortem examination. The aim is to provide a documented interpretation of the events and their sequence, at the site of killing and burial.[1]

My work in forensic archaeology demonstrates how the recovery of bodies has recovered history, affirming the fragile and contested memory of atrocity, with consequence not only for contemporary understanding, but also for justice. Justice and its formal requirements affected the process of recovery and analysis of the bodies and their places of internment. In the cases of Serniki and Ustinovka in the Ukraine and Kozluk, Glogova, Medak, and

---

[1] R. Wright, I. Hanson, and J. Sterenberg, "Mass grave excavation," in *Forensic Archaeology: Advances in Theory and Practice,* ed. J. Hunter and M. Cox (London: Routledge, 2005), 137-58.

Srebrenica in Bosnia and Croatia, court inquiries presented questions of consistency with memory of events, body identity, and causes and times of bodies' demise that required evidence of past events that bodies could provide. Legal purposes also meant active contestation in Bosnian and Croatian cases from defendant "revisionists" who presented alternative stories, denying our archaeological analysis and conclusions in public and in court. Attention to detail, as well as confirmation with oral, aerial, and other sources was therefore integral to the archaeological recovery and interpretation of the bodies. And in the end, archaeology enabled the bodies to resist revision and recover history.

Both evidentiary and humanitarian archaeology need archaeological work done to high standards. This is no methodological platitude. If historians misinterpret a document, then another historian can put matters right by reinterpreting the document. By contrast if I, as a forensic archaeologist, misinterpret a mass grave, then I have destroyed it by the very act of excavating it. I have put the grave itself beyond further examination. So forensic archaeological work must be done to high standards.[2]

Yet there is a difference between evidentiary and humanitarian forensic archaeology, which affects the psychology of the archaeologist. This is so because evidentiary forensic archaeology will be severely cross-examined, which forces concentration on the recording of the excavation and the implications that has for a reconstruction of what went on there. In evidentiary archaeology there is no room for the flights of reconstructive fancy that characterize many archaeological reports.

For example, Mortimer Wheeler excavated at the Iron Age hillfort of Maiden Castle in the 1930s. He imaginatively interpreted bones as representing British people killed by the Roman invaders.[3] It is doubtful that Wheeler's interpretations would stand up to cross-examination in a court. When the evidence was examined again by Sharples,[4] he found that what Wheeler interpreted as a war cemetery included a predominance of skeletons that showed no injuries and had been buried with careful Iron Age ritual, including grave goods.[5]

The same concentration should also be applied to humanitarian archaeology, since it is important for evidence that might help identification not to be lost. Nevertheless in humanitarian work thankful relatives rarely ask the penetrating questions that resemble aggressive cross-examination in forensic archaeological work.

The challenge and importance of the work pulled me into forensic archaeology—into practice that answers the question "where are the bodies?" In January 1990 the Special Investigations Unit (the SIU) of the Australian Attorney General's Department was looking into the cases of three men in Adelaide. It was alleged that they had killed some hundreds of Jews in Ukraine in 1942, after Nazi occupation of the area. The SIU wanted to know if there was material evidence in the ground for one of these killings. Was there a mass grave at a place called Serniki in northwestern Ukraine? If so, what were its properties?

They approached Dr. Godfrey Oettle, pathologist at the New South Wales Institute of Forensic Medicine, to ask whether he would be prepared to find and excavate the supposed mass grave at Serniki. He was told that there was an eyewitness to the murders. As a youth of 16, the eyewitness was one of several local youths the Nazi Einsatzgruppen forced to refill the grave. The eyewitness said the grave was some 50 meters long, 5 meters wide, and 2-3 meters deep. It contained up to 800 bodies and was probably dug to below the local water table.

Locating and excavating such a site promised to be a formidable job. Dr. Oettle had the professional good sense to say to the SIU that he was a pathologist and that Serniki was a job for an archaeologist. I had been excavating for Late Pleistocene archaeology in spring-fed swamps in New South Wales, and so he

[2] M. Cox, A. Flavel, I. Hanson, J. Laver, and R. Wessling, *The Scientific Investigation of Mass Graves* (Cambridge: Cambridge University Press, 2008).

[3] M. Wheeler, *Maiden Castle, Dorset.* Reports of the Research Committee of the Society of Antiquaries of London 12 (London: Oxford University Press, 1943).

[4] N. Sharples, *Maiden Castle* (London: Batsford, 1991).

[5] Ibid.

suggested my name. The SIU approached me and I jumped at the offer to do this extraordinary work in Ukraine.

Godfrey's professional judgment was right. The work of pathologists is primarily in the laboratory, examining human remains and determining the cause and manner of death. They are not professionally trained for archaeological fieldwork, and so are likely to be objected to as proper expert witnesses in court, if presenting critical archaeological testimony.

In order to prepare evidence for cross-examination, the discovery and excavation of a mass grave requires that the archaeologist must know how to address logistics issues such as estimating how long the job will take and what resources are needed, how to dig a deep pit safely in sand, how to control groundwater in a wet soil environment, how to run a team of diggers, and how to manage dangerous machinery, as well as addressing research issues including how to record evidence three dimensionally and how to read in the soil the stratigraphy of original burial and later disturbance.

The work of preparing for cross-examination went beyond routine archaeological fieldwork. Certainly evidentiary work at the Serniki mass grave was more challenging than any archaeology I had done before 1990. I enlisted my wife Sonia, a field archaeologist, and with her as my field assistant we excavated Serniki and two more mass graves in the Ukraine in 1990 and 1991 for the SIU.

Many of the SIU prosecutors and investigators moved on to take part in international war crimes investigations with the International Criminal Tribunal for the Former Yugoslavia (ICTY) in The Hague. Six years later, I joined them to work in Bosnia. I would serve as their Chief Archaeologist from 1997 until 2000. The investigations in the Ukraine and the former Yugoslavia show how international justice inquiries sought to answer the question "Where are the bodies?" They allow us to assess the role of forensic archaeology in testing the statements of eyewitnesses and survivors of mass murder and burial.

Without the bodies as material evidence of events such as the Holocaust, those who wish to deny that they happened can—and have tried hard to—set up a contest where we argue about how to interpret words in historical documents, and about the integrity of the characters and memories of those who claim to remember. Of course historical scholarship and memories are critical, but the powerful evidence of the bodies themselves, especially in conjunction with documentary evidence and witness memory, is difficult to contest. If bodies with gunshots are there in the ground, then somebody shot them. The bodies demand an explanation. In the Ukrainian and Bosnian cases, those explanations, and thus the bodies, gained historical meaning through the practiced eye and objective research processes of forensic professionals.

How right was the sixteen-year-old witness of Serniki in his memories of that ghastly event? His recollection led the archaeological team to the grave, which turned out to contain some 550 bodies and not the 800 he had estimated. The grave was also some 10 m shorter than he said. But these were small discrepancies to be held against the memories of a lad under stress, and the excavation demonstrated the power of bodies to bear out his recollection in other ways.

More specifically, the witness said that we would find a ramp on one side of the grave, down which the Jews were herded before being made to lie down like sardines and shot in the back of the head. At the base of the ramp he said we would find the bodies of those who were brought to the grave after the main mass of the murdered had been shot. These residual few had been mostly clubbed to death. We found these claims about the Serniki grave to be materialized in the soil—namely the general size and shape of the grave, the fact that there were hundreds of bodies in it, the two types of disposition of the bodies, and the manner of death.[6]

Having found the bodies in Serniki, in 1991 we turned to excavation of the site of Ustinovka in Ukraine, where it was alleged that some 150 adults were killed and buried in a mass grave in 1942. The police chief, under orders from the Germans, was

---

[6] For a general review of the Serniki case see D. Bevan, *A Case to Answer* (Kent Town, South Australia: Wakefield Press, 1994).

The whole length of the mass grave at Serniki in Ukraine, the murders dating from 1942 and excavated in 1991. (Photo by Richard Wright)

commandeered a cart, put some 20 children into it, and drove the cart up to the grave. The chief then threw the children in and shot those whose necks were not broken.

Our excavation supported the statements of eyewitnesses to these atrocious events at Ustinovka. We found the bodies of the children first, ranging between six months and twelve years old at their deaths. The surface on which the children lay higgledy-piggledy looked at first like the base of the grave. However further probing showed that this supposed base was in fact soil that had been thrown back over the adults below.

In Ustinovka, archaeology not only supported the statement of eyewitnesses, but it also elaborated their statements. None had mentioned that the grave was partly refilled, merely that there was an interval of time between the killing of the adults and the killing of the children. Archaeology tested the oral testimony, confirmed it, and supplemented the initial inquiry with evidence of bodies that addressed further atrocity.

The recovery of bodies can reveal more, showing evidence of acts after mass killings intended to keep bodies from being found, as I learned in 1998 while working for ICTY in Bosnia. There we found a grave that was "secondary." In other words the evidence showed that the bodies had been dug up elsewhere

said to have complained to his lieutenant that the children of mixed marriage (Jewish and Gentile) were not brought to him for killing. So the chief ordered his deputy back to the village, where he

The murdered children of Ustinovka, the murders dating from 1942 and excavated in 1992. (Photo by Richard Wright)

(the primary grave) and brought to the secondary grave. There were two important indicators of the grave being secondary—bodies were dismembered, and artifacts in the grave were out of geographical context. We found thousands of fragments of green glass that had been trucked in with the bodies.

Some fragments had the name of a bottling factory at Kozluk, a town some thirty minutes drive to the northeast. The evidence of the bottles compelled me to suggest to ICTY that there must have been a place of execution and burial in the town of Kozluk—a primary grave at a place where the bottling factory dumped their broken bottles. The green glass in the secondary grave we were examining must have been transferred there with the bodies. I asked myself, had the perpetrators retrieved all the bodies from the primary grave? If not, where were the bodies?

In 2000 we searched for the factory's bottle dump at Kozluk. There we found a glass-strewn slope smothered with some 300 bodies that the perpetrators failed to remove for reburial in secondary graves. The bodies had been covered up with soil dredged from the nearby river.

This discovery was of such significance that the Prosecutor of ICTY was helicoptered in. She wanted to see for herself the bodies and associated evidence, bodies that demonstrated an elaborate effort to evade investigation and recovery.

Finding the bodies took a similar course in the case of the Kravica warehouse killings and mass grave in Glogova. In 1998 some six hundred men and boys were murdered by the Bosnian Serb military while packed into the Kravica warehouse in Bosnia. The military used grenades and machine guns. Remarkably there was a survivor, therefore an eyewitness, who escaped from under the pile of murdered bodies. He said that after the killings the door of the warehouse was broken down to allow a front-end loader to get in and scoop up some bodies. They were taken away in trucks. At nightfall the removal stopped, leaving him still among the pile of bodies. He said that grass was put over the bodies—he thought to set fire to them, but probably to hide them from UN patrols that were in the area. During the night the eyewitness escaped through a window in the warehouse.

The warehouse was empty when the investigators had a look a few months later, though body tissue was still embedded in the walls. Where were the bodies? One possibility was seemingly disturbed ground at Glogova, some 10 km to the east. My team went there in 2000. We found, as at Kozluk, that most of the bodies had been taken away by the perpetrators trying to hide the evidence. Again, as at Kozluk, we had found a secondary grave before the primary one. Significantly, among the undisturbed

Bodies on the glass-strewn slope at Kozluk, in Bosnia, the murders dating from 1995 and excavated in 1999. (Photo courtesy of ICTY)

bodies at Glogova we found hay, plastic cladding from the Kravica warehouse walls, and almost the complete door and frame that had been broken down to let in the front-end loader. As at Ustinovka in Ukraine, archaeology had tested oral evidence and added to the detail of that evidence.

Archaeology can also test denials of past events as they are revised to explain evidence found on the bodies. Another investigation in the former Yugoslavia demonstrated this vividly; in the case of the Medak area in Croatia, I witnessed this sort of evolving denial and its exposure by excavation. An eyewitness had said that Croatian soldiers had killed Serb civilians in 1993. The witness said the bodies were taken to an unused and open cesspit at a half-built house. The walls of the house were blown up, so that the rubble fell into and over the cesspit.

Investigating the acts of a standing government presented special challenges to investigators. With massive protection from the Croatian police, special forces, and secret service, we set about excavating this cesspit. The agreement with ICTY was that a Croatian official could witness everything we did. The official lectured us on the first day—we were wasting our time. The cesspit, if it contained any bodies at all, would contain the bodies of Serb soldiers. The official monitored our excavation over two weeks.

One day my excavators reported finding plaits of hair among bones in the cesspit. The official asserted it was well known that Serb soldiers wore plaits. Then we found the shoulder part of what resembled a smart evening dress. As soon as the shoulder of the dress turned up, I asked my Indian heavy equipment driver, who spoke fluent Serbo-Croatian, to go and stand by the official and the advisor to find out what they were saying. "Now we could have a problem," was what he reported the official as saying.

Bodies present danger to those who would revise the past. Perpetrators of violence are forced to make contorted efforts to protect their position once the material evidence begins to emerge. Having to deal with bodies tests their ingenuity. Before bodies are found, for example, such revisionists often deny that there are any bodies. When bodies are found, the numbers are said to be too few to show that a

massacre took place. Where the numbers found are adequate to suggest a massacre, then revisionists argue that the bodies are due to unrelated events—for example are the result of cleaning up the landscape after soldiers were killed in battle.[7]

What happened in the investigation of the Srebrenica massacre is perhaps the most prominent example of the importance to history of the presence of bodies. The Srebrenica killing took place in July 1995. Some 7,500 men and teenage boys were separated from the women and children, and taken away in buses and trucks. They were not seen again. Where were their bodies?

In 1996, some attempts to find bodies had been made by ICTY, not using a team led by archaeologists. The group thought that at one site the supposed mass graves contained many fewer bodies than contemporary accounts suggested. We now know, following detailed archaeological work, that this site had been virtually emptied out in places by the perpetrators, and this effect was not originally noticed by the exhumation team as cuts into the stratification of the grave filling—these cuts being evidence that digging had taken place after burial. At the time, the apparent absence of bodies was important, affecting credibility of the charge. As *Newsweek* reporter Stacy Sullivan asked: "Genocide without corpses: Srebrenica was said to be Europe's biggest atrocity since World War II. So why haven't more bodies been found?"[8]

By an integrated study of aerial imagery dating from 1995 and forensic archaeology, we found the bodies. In October 1995, three months after the massacre, the perpetrators had exhumed the primary graves, trucked the putrefying bodies into remote country, and reburied them in a series of secondary graves. Clearly, they were trying to hide the evidence from UN investigators.

Aerial imagery (which I believe was merely routine mass coverage) subsequently revealed their

---

[7] A review of revisionism is contained in E. S. Herman, "The Approved Narrative of the Srebrenica Massacre," *International Journal for the Semiotics of Law* 19, no. 4, (2006): 409-34.

[8] *Newsweek*, November 4, 1996.

attempts to hide the evidence. Using this aerial imagery and archaeological methods, we were able to work out from the secondary graves we excavated which primary grave the bodies came from. We discovered evidence such as the transfer of soil, artifacts, crops, and fruit. Our work from 1998-2000 accounted for some five thousand bodies, all the result of the Srebrenica massacre. Some of these five thousand were left by us in graves that we merely probed. Since then, humanitarian work has recovered them—and many hundreds more from other graves.

The bodies demonstrated, in my opinion, that these people were not killed in battle as the revisionists and defense counsel argued. In the first place I saw no military clothing. Even if soldiers had changed to civilian clothes before being killed, why were most of them wearing ligatures of cloth tying their hands behind their backs, or wearing blindfolds, or wearing both? It is a war crime to murder prisoners.

Finally, there was some exquisite detail exposed by my archaeological team that linked the people back to the Srebrenica massacre. There was Dutch newspaper cut to cigarette paper size in pockets of some murdered individuals. The Dutch had been the UN contingent in Srebrenica when it was besieged and at the time it fell. There were self-winding Seiko watches that show the day and date, and stop some 36-48 hours after movement. Eight out of ten of the watches found in the mass graves showed a day/date combination that was consistent with the supposed date of execution.

Through locating and recovering the bodies, we now know what happened in 1995. The perpetrators shot the victims in July, buried them in mass graves, and then dug them up in October 1995 in a vain attempt to hide the evidence of the original massacre. Ironically, by doing this they added to the charges that were brought against them by the prosecution at ICTY. Attempting to hide evidence of a crime is itself a crime.

Because bodies are such powerful historical and legal evidence, the defenders of alleged perpetrators have added interrogation of investigators' research and recovery processes to their cross-examination.

That attempt at distraction should not surprise. For example, David Bright of the University of New South Wales,[9] and news media have pointed out the effects of evidence such as gruesome photos on courts.[10]

In the case of atrocity investigations, forensic archaeologists present to the courts detailed logs and maps of what is found, with interpretations. Official reports, which include photos, are disclosed to the defense. In accord with Bright's findings, usually the defense does not want the judges to see the gruesome pictures. So the reports are unchallenged by defense counsel. The defense prefers to argue the line of "you prove that our client was seen pulling the trigger." That has happened in most cases that I have worked on.

Yet the Srebrenica defense teams also devised a strategy to question whether, because of our supposed preconceptions, our archaeological investigation missed identifying military clothing, and whether the number of bodies in the ground was less than we estimated.[11] I have vivid memories of a grueling cross-examination in The Hague in February 2007. On and on went the questions about the possibility of my being mistaken in my observations and conclusions. I insisted that I had not seen an item of military clothing on the 2000-3000 bodies my team had exhumed. I insisted that I was not mistaken in seeing high numbers of blindfolds and arms tied behind the back. Words, words, words from both

---

[9] D. A. Bright, "Gruesome Evidence and Emotion: Anger, Blame, and Jury Decision-Making," *Law and Human Behavior* 30 (2006): 83-202.

[10] *Sydney Morning Herald,* November 17, 2007.

[11] The ICTY trial transcripts are accessible on the Web. They give a vivid insight into questions of "where are the bodies." The two cases of Krstic and Popovic *et al.* are the most relevant to what I have written. To access these transcripts visit http://www.un.org/icty/cases-e/index-e.htm. For the Krstic case search the page for IT-98-33. This search will take you to Krstic (IT-98-33) "Srebrenica-Drina Corps." Click on Transcripts. For the case of Popovic *et al.* search the page for IT-05-88. This search will take you to Popovic et al. (IT-05-88). Click on Transcripts.

myself and the defense team of barristers. In his right of reply the prosecuting barrister said nothing; he simply put up two photos on the court's screen.

They were the photos from my official report of a man in civilian clothes, who had broken the ligature fixing his hands behind his back, slipped his blindfold down, and grasped a shrub at the moment of death. The prosecuting barrister asked me a single question. Were these photos the sort of evidence that led me to my conclusions. I said yes. The prosecuting barrister said he had no more questions for me. I think that the photos of a body cut through the verbiage of the courtroom, effectively arresting the defense efforts to reinterpret the evidence. Verdicts are awaited as I am writing this.

Bodies are frightening, and not wanting to find and see them does at times deflect investigators from answering the question "Where are the bodies?" This deflection weakens investigations. It is at this point that forensic archaeologists can help concentrate the investigations. Finding bodies can be disturbing, but is obviously not distasteful to these professionals, especially given the purpose of their work.

It is perhaps further testimony to the power of bodies that for some, the encounter with bodies has raised the question of whether our work is psychologically disturbing to ourselves. How do I feel about uncovering the dead and the evil context in which they lie? The work is often technically challenging, absorbing, dangerous and disgusting—but frankly it is not distressing—not emotionally distressing in a way that would keep a psychological counselor in business.[12] Yet current practice often requires counseling of professionals in my line of work. It can be disruptive, but more importantly I believe that it is worth asking what the consequences of that might become for our professional purpose: can the very

presence of counselors imply that we have undergone some sort of appalling stress by dealing with the bodies that affects the work? Or that because we have not undergone emotional stress, our work might be suspect?

It is important to the understanding of the work of the forensic archaeologist, and clear to me, that in this work we have not undergone traumatic stress. We have not had sudden and unexpected emotional trauma. We are not like a member of the public who has had to rescue a burning child from a car containing its incinerated parents. We start each job prepared for the worst and the worst develops slowly. This is not to say one lacks emotional moments, but they are a release and not a sign of psychological damage.

Emotions can come out when the bodies in the ground become personalized. I experienced this in working on the Srebrenica massacre at the site of Glogova. I had already worked for four years in Bosnia, and it was ten years after beginning my work at Serniki. One day at Glogova we opened a wallet found with a body, a once living person reduced to a pair of jeans and a denim jacket, both filled with shattered bones, putrefying flesh, and hair. Inside the wallet was a license with a color photo of the fresh-faced young owner of the wallet. I looked at his date of birth on the document and said to my scene-of-crime officer, "This lad is the same age as my daughter ... I mean *was* the same age." That "was the same age" grabbed my throat. I could not speak. I had to take deep breaths and go for a walk around an abandoned orchard before returning to work. Merging the murdered lad with my own family had distressed me. But rather than endangering me or the work, I believe the recognition affirmed my well being and reinforced for me the purpose of the difficult work of recovering the bodies.

In summary, answering the question "Where are the bodies" leads forensic archaeologists to recover evidence that disturbs people. Lawyers know that the evidence disturbs other people, including jurors and judges. Revisionists know the bodies must be smothered to protect their interests. This suggests that finding the bodies of victims of atrocities is important, essential to contemporary justice as well as

---

[12] Something of the psycho-social environment of forensic archaeological work is given in R. Wright and I. Hanson, "How to do forensic archaeology under the auspices of large organizations like the United Nations" in *Handbook of Forensic Archaeology and Anthropology*, ed. S. Blau and D. Ubelaker (California: Left Coast Press, 2008), 468-78.

to historical accuracy and understanding. My experiences in the Ukraine, Bosnia, and Croatia confirm that. They also show that the effort of perpetrators and supporters to explain away bodies and an accurate understanding of the past does not end once the bodies are found. That makes the forensic work of investigating the bodies as important as locating and recovering them.

Sadly, the investigation of mass graves is not a calling that will end soon. People continue to kill en masse. So it is a good thing that the forensic archaeologist remains sane, even if the rest of the world needs counseling.

RICHARD WRIGHT is emeritus professor of anthropology at the University of Sydney. In 1990-91 he conducted excavations into mass graves of the Holocaust in Ukraine. From 1997 to 2000 he was chief archaeologist for the UN's investigations of mass graves in Bosnia. Currently (2009) he is senior forensic adviser for Oxford Archaeology's task of recovering and identifying bodies from World War I mass graves at Fromelles, in northeast France.

The author acknowledges the assistance of a multitude of people who helped get this forensic archaeology properly finished. Because they run into the hundreds, to name a few would be invidious.

Chapter 3

Primates

Students often wonder why we study monkeys and apes in a class that is supposed to be about humans. Of course, humans are primates, and we have a lot in common with the other 250+ different species of primates found around the world. The study of primates helps us better understand various aspects of human biology, because we share so much of our DNA and body structure with primates. Primates see and experience the world pretty much the same way we do, and their complex brains allow them to engage in sophisticated social groups. Many primates are also tool users, an activity we once thought was isolated to humans.

We also study primates because they are interesting in their own right, apart from what they may be able to tell us about ourselves. They form parts of complex ecosystems, and understanding their roles in the environment can help us better understand how both they, and the various environments they are found in, have evolved over time.

Sadly, many primate species are highly endangered and threatened with extinction. There are many reasons for this problem, but habitat destruction and overhunting by humans are high on the list of threats to many primate species. It is probable that

several different primates will be extinct by the end of this decade; even some great apes like the mountain gorilla and orangutan could become extinct in the wild during your lifetime if we cannot reverse these trends.

Since Jane Goodall's work from the 1960s, anthropologists have used the knowledge gained from watching nonhuman primates to better understand human behavior, and the possible behaviors and social interactions exhibited by our early hominid ancestors.

The articles in this section of the reader will help introduce you to several different types of primates in more detail than you will find in the textbook. In "Dance of the Sexes," you will read about the sexual politics of the sifaka, a type of prosimian on Madagascar. "Married to the Mob" provides an in-depth look at some surprising behaviors seen in tarsiers. "Family Feuds" looks at differing strategies for reproductive success in howler monkeys. And "Aping Culture" looks at the wide diversity of behaviors seen in different groups of chimpanzees, and how that diversity may signal the beginnings of what we humans would recognize as culture.

Family Feuds

By Carolyn M. Cockett

Conflict and even infanticide are part of red howler monkey society, and both affect female reproductive success.

One evening in July 1979, while checking on one of the troops of red howler monkeys I had been studying in Venezuela, I noticed something odd. The troop had split up into two groups, which were sleeping in trees about seventy-five yards apart. This division was very unusual for howlers, especially in this habitat—an open, shrubby grassland, with few tall trees. When I looked closely at the smaller faction, I saw an adult female that was sitting on a branch with her two sons; she had deep, fresh wounds on her face. A second adult female that was with the larger group also had cuts on her face and arm. And her twenty-month-old daughter was missing,

The next morning, the first adult female made her way back to the main group. Her hair standing on end, she rapidly approached and grabbed the second female and began harassing her. The two monkeys howled loudly at each other, but the hostilities soon subsided. By afternoon, the injuries were the only evidence that anything had happened between them. However, the second female's daughter did not return.

About two months later, I saw the missing, youngster again. She had joined a newly fomed troop a few hundred yards to the west of he troop she was born into. Her departure from her natal troop affirmed a pattern we have been seeing in our census data since 196. In this pattern, which has a profound effect on the lives and reproductive strategies of females, both female and male red howler monkeys emigrate from their natal troops. Furthermore, circumstantial evidence suggests that conflict among females themselves is largely responsible for the emigration of young females. I suspect, for example, that the twenty-month-old female left her home troop because she was forced out after her mother had lost a fight with the other adult female.

The red howler monkeys of Hato Masaguaral, the Venezuelan wildlife pre-serve and cattle ranch where I have been conducting my research, have been studied for a number of years. Melvin Neville, now of Loyola University, did the pioneering fieldwork on this population in 1969. In the mid-1970s, researchers from the Smithsonian Institution began several field projects at the ranch.

The red howler monkey (*Atouatta seniculus*) is one of six howler species distributed from southern Mexico to northern Argentina. Red howler monkeys have the largest geographical distribution of the *Alouatta* and are found throughout much of South America north of the Amazon River and into Bolivia in the west. Red howlers reside from sea level to more than 7,000 feet in the Andes. More remarkably, not only do they range in evergreen rain forests but they also occur at even higher densities in the highly seasonal, semi-deciduous habitats of Hato Masaguaral. Since red howler monkeys do not need to drink water, they can survive in scrubby areas far from streams.

Like other howler monkeys, red howlers are vegetarians. They eat leaves, fruits, and flowers and seem to prefer ephemeral food items such as tender young leaves and ripe fruits. Much of their food is relatively unnutritious, and they must eat large amounts to meet their caloric needs. Perhaps as a consequence, they are inactive for much of the time, apparently digesting their bulky diet. This lethargy means that howlers do little other than sleep, eat, and travel to sleeping and feeding places. Social interactions are infrequent compared with those of more frenetic monkey species. However, red howler monkeys do one thing particularly vigorously—they howl. Howling, or more descriptively, "roaring," is usually a troop affair, with adults and larger imrnatures of both sexes participating. Males have a bigger vocal apparatus than females; their roars are deeper and louden. Troops frequently howl at dawn, pausing internittently to listen to the calls of neighboring troops. During the daytime, troops often howl when they encounter one another. Red howler troops' home ranges overlap somewhat with those of their neighbors, and intertroop interactions usually take place in the area of overlap. During these interactions juveniles of the opposing troops sometimes play vigorously. Occasionally one troop will suddenly charge, driving the opposing troop into another tree.

For years, howlers were characterized as peaceful and nonaggressive, even though they were sometimes seen with serious wounds. These were usually ascribed to unsuccessful predators. As with many animal studies, years passed before we could determine what was really going on. We now know that, while infrequent and seldom observed, violent fighting sometimes erupts. Many researchers have come to believe that reproductive competition is usually the cause.

Red howler troops average about nine individuals, with one to two adult males, two to four adult females, and various immatures. Thus, the adult sex ratio of this polygynous species is about two females per male. Typically larger than adult females, adult males compete with each other for entry into troops and access to females. As a result, they clash violently and occasionally kill each other. Assailants often invade a troop in pairs, and these cooperating males have greater success in expelling resident males than single invaders do. Male invasions and takeovers are dramatic events, which may be why studies of nonhuman primates have emphasized male behavior. Females were often neglected in earlier studies, except for studies of mother-infant interactions. That females' lives might also be shaped by reproductive competition is a relatively new focus for field studies. An interest in this subject is part of what brought me to Venezuela in October 1978.

When I arrived, Rudy Rudran of the Smithsonian Institution helped orient me to the area and to observing the monkeys, which by then were already accustomed to humans. (Rudran had been censusing red howler troops living in the open habitat of the ranch since 1976.) The following March, I began a two-year study, accompanied and assisted in numerous ways by my husband, Bob Brooks.

One of my first objectives was to expand the red howler project to a second habitat, a gallery forest about two and a half miles east of the open woodland site. The forest is also semi-deciduous and its canopy is higher and more closed than that of the woodland study area. I eventually located twenty-five red howler monkey troops in this sometimes impenetrable forest, and added seven more from the open woodland censused by Rudran. Together with the twenty troops he was already monitoring, this made fifty-two troops under observations. After the end of the two-year study, I censused them again three times. In addition to keeping track of the individual members of these troops, I studied the social behavior and feeding ecology of one troop from each habitat.

But the tendency of females to emigrate was what interested me most. Female emigration is uncommon in most primate species (but see *Natural History* articles for September 1981—Chapter 1 in this volume—and for March 1982—Chapter 2 in this volume—about emigration by female red colobus and gorillas). About one in five females and, apparently, a very few males grow up and reproduce in their natal troops, but most do not.

A troop of red howler monkeys, Alouatta seniculus, join in a group howl. Troops frequently howl at each other, particularly in the early morning, to sound out their locations.

Between October 1978 and December 1981, twenty-nine immature females and thirty-three young males left their known or presumed natal troops. I could not be certain of the fates of all of them, but a minimum of one-third survived for at least a while after emigration. (It is difficult to determine how many disappearances are deaths and how many are dispersals.) One thing became very clear, however. Emigrant males had much greater success in subsequently entering established troops than did females. During the period that twenty males immigrated into established troops, only two females had the same luck.

Fortunately, joining an established troop is not an emigrant female's only option. Red howlers also form new troops, with other expatriated males and females. We call a group of monkeys a troop once one of the females gives birth, and I refer to troops that have been around for awhile as established to distinguish them from newly formed troops. Furthermore, I apply the term first-generation to those troops formed from unrelated female monkeys; once the offspring of these females begin reproducing, I call them multiple-generation troops.

All of this jargon has arisen because an astounding number of new troops have formed at Hato Masaguaral in the past few years. Between 1979 and 1984, seven new troops formed in the open woodland study area and thirteen troops formed in the less populated gallery forest. Both study areas are of similar size, about one and one-half square miles.

The incipient troop must find a suitable piece of real estate to use as its home range. Some new troops that couldn't do so eventually dissolved, and their members dispersed. In the higher-density open woodland, about 60 percent of primiparous, or first-time, births were to females in their natal troops. In the gallery forest, the pattern was very different: 84 percent of prirniparous births were to females in newly formed troops, because so many more new troops were able to form there.

Thus, one way an emigrating female can survive is to form a new troop with others. But she doesn't always get such a chance immediately, and a monkey that is "looking" for such a spot may be more vulnerable than monkeys already in troops. For example, solitary females may starve or be preyed upon by pumas or caimans, although we haven't unequivocally documented that monkeys at Hato Masaguaral have died for either of these reasons. Some young female monkeys stay on the fringes of their natal troops, but others begin to wander and may end up in habitats far from their birthplace, and not nearly as hospitable. Once I saw a young adult female walking beside an irrigation canal next to the highway, at least two miles from the nearest suitable habitat. This was a particularly strange sight because howlers usually spend as little time as possible on the ground and cross rapidly from one clump of vegetation to another. Another female, born in an open woodland troop, disappeared for more than a year before turning up in a gallery forest troop nearly four miles from her birthplace. Howlers that don't disperse spend their lives in small ranges about 300 to 600 yards across.

Another drawback for emigrant females is that, while waiting to join a troop, they may delay their first pregnancies. A female that emigrates at two to four years of age might lead an extratroop existence for several years without reproducing (females become sexually mature at age four to five). Such a female is at an evolutionary disadvantage compared with females that breed earlier. The first strike against her as a late breeder is that she may produce fewer total offspring. Furthermore, her genes will be represented later in the next generation because the young she does produce will mature later, on average, than offspring of females that breed younger. Since fitness is defined as the proportion of genes an individual contributes to future generations, later-reproducing monkeys lose out.

Ranka Sekulic, who studied the howling and ranging patterns of four red howler troops on the ranch, documented a young adult female's fruitless attempts to join an established troop in September 1979. In December 1981, I found that this female was still dogging the same troop. By this time, she must have been about seven years old and still had not reproduced. Finally, in February 1984, I saw her in a newly formed troop with an infant.

Overall, I estimate that of all females born, about 20 percent breed in their natal troops, while about 6 percent breed in nonnatal troops that they joined or formed in the study area. (About 25 percent die before two years of age.) The rest disappear—some die and others disperse undetected to locations beyond the study area, where a portion may succeed in breeding.

If emigrating poses such risks for a female, why should she emigrate at all? Why do some young monkeys stay in their natal troops while others emigrate? The answer may be that some females do not have a choice. Red howler troop size appears to be limited possibly because of a restricted food supply on a given home range. At Hato Masaguaral, troops average about nine individuals; the largest I counted had eighteen. Perhaps more important, the number of adult females is limited. Of sixty-five troops I have counted, none had more than four adult females, and about 90 percent had only two or three. These numbers are not explainable by mortality rates— more females are born than die.

What this implies is that females compete for breeding positions in their natal troops. One might assume that mothers would fight to keep their daughters in the home troop, but this is not necessarily true. If, for example, resources are scarce, both mothers and daughters may have more to gain if the daughter leaves and joins a new troop in an area with more plentiful food. In other cases, there may be a conflict, either between mother and daughter or among the adult mothers, all of which may favor keeping their own daughters in the troop rather than the daughters of the others. The competition over daughters may be particularly intense when the adult females are not related to each other, as is the case in first-generation troops—conflicts among females occasionally escalate to physical fights. Although I have never actually observed a fight in which an adult female was injured, many adult and subadult females have permanent scars or were seen with serious injuries at some point during the study. In several instances I observed females with fresh injuries, apparently shortly after a fight. In these cases, the females were still behaving aggressively by vocalizing, grabbing, and generally hassling one another. Red howlers seem to avoid expending unnecessary energy, and their low rate of social interaction may explain why so few fights are actually witnessed. Thus, I have had to infer some female-female aggression from injuries. In nearly all cases, these injuries coincided with emigrations of young females or their ultimate acceptance as reproductive adults.

In the troop I observed in the gallery forest, the young daughter of one of the resident females often picked fights with the other adult female and her son. In these interactions, the young female would grab the fingers, shoulders, or head of her rival, attempting to harass the other red howler the same way young males sometimes harass adult males. Another way the young female and the adult showed hostility toward each other was to toss their heads in a kind of synchronous, mimetic rhythm. Some of these interactions were provoked by the adult female, when the young female and her mother were close together. Typically, she grimaced widely and gave a loud, "cackling" vocalization that lasted more than a minute.

Eventually, however, the conflict was resolved. The young female was allowed to stay and become a reproducing female in her naval troop. The intense interactions declined in frequency after that; to me this was evidence that what I had witnessed was a struggle over the fate of the daughter, one that is typical of the conflicts among female red howler monkeys.

But as with the twenty-month-old female monkey that emigrated and joined a "new" troop, the daughter does not always get to stay. This does not mean, however, that she is always gone for good. That same female monkey left her new troop about a year after joining it. In January 1981, we captured and ear tagged her several hundred yards away from her natal troop. That same month, the first adult female of the troop—the one I believe drove the juvenile out—died. Within one month of that death, the juvenile was back in her natal range, and two months after that she had rejoined her original troop and was spending much time near her mother. This supports my conclusion that her original emigration was not entirely "voluntary" and may have been precipitated by the other resident female.

Emigration by primates is often explained as a way to avoid incest, because inbreeding can cause birth defects. Since red howler males commonly leave their home troops, females usually do not need to emigrate to avoid mating with relatives. Also, many breeding males have been replaced by new males by the time their daughters reach sexual maturity. So females probably emigrate because the number of breeding positions within a troop is limited, and breeding opportunities can be found in the outside world.

Whether she remains in her natal troop or emigrates, a female's problems are not over even after she has made the crucial crossing into adulthood. She still has to protect any young she bears from males attempting to invade her troop and depose the resident males. These invasions are highly correlated with infant mortality: there is strong evidence that males that take over troops kill young infants, then mate with their mothers.

I have not observed infanticide, but both Rudran and Sekulic have seen it at Hato Masaguaral, and Margaret Clarke has reported that infanticide occurs among mantled howlers (*A. palliata*) in Costa Rica. Since 1979, more than twenty red howler infants in my study area have vanished under circumstances that probably involved infanticide. In five cases, the disappearance occurred shortly after an invading male was seen stalking the mother and infant. In other cases, the disappearances generally coincided with changes in male membership, either when new males took over or when a formerly subordinate male ousted the male that had previously mated with the females.

In at least six instances, infant red howler monkeys conceived under an old regime, but born after a change in male membership, vanished within two to three weeks after birth. Sarah Blaffer Hrdy, who has studied Hanuman langurs (*Presbytis entellus*), Asian monkeys that also commit infanticide, believes that females of the species have evolved the strategy of faking estrus to deceive new males about the paternity of already-conceived young as a way of protecting them. In other words, a pregnant female langur displays estrous behavior, soliciting the male, and as a result, the male who mates with her may "believe" that the infant born later is his. Because female red howlers appear to be unable to feign estrus, infants conceived prior to the time of a takeover are just as likely to disappear as those already born.

When Sekulic and I analyzed this quantitatively, we found that infanticide victims were at just the age that we would expect if they were being killed by males seeking a reproductive advantage. Red howler infancy lasts about one year. However, infants believed to be infanticide victims have all been under ten months of age. Since red howler females give birth on the average of every 16.6 months (presuming that the previous infant survives), and the gestation period is about 6.3 months, females with infants older than nine months are likely to be pregnant again already, so killing their current infants would have no effect on their ability to conceive. But females with younger infants are less likely to be pregnant; therefore, infanticide could result in an early return to estrus. Females do indeed conceive sooner after losing infants; the average interbirth interval then is reduced to 10.5 months. By killing infants, males may mate sooner. Furthermore, since his tenure as breeding male is relatively short and unpredictable, the sooner the male produces his own offspring, the more likely they are to survive. After all, he too can be deposed, making his offspring vulnerable to the next male.

In short, infanticidal males have greater reproductive success than noninfanticidal males. Any genes affecting infanticidal behavior can be transmitted to the males' offspring, and the behavior can become widespread. Thus, infanticide can be viewed as adaptive for red howler males, since they seem to kill only in circumstances where it gives them a reproductive edge.

But what about red howler females? They are clearly losers. Since they cannot fake estrus, what can females do to defend against infanticide? They can, and do, try to avoid new males if they already have young. I have seen females, along with other members of their troop, chasing interlopers, a tactic that may forestall infanticide, but one that is not particularly successful in the long run. Of the infants I studied, only 25 percent survived a change in male membership unscathed. A few of the survivors have received serious injuries. Since the odds are against the survival of her current son or daughter, and one she may be carrying, a female's usual strategy after an infant dies is to conceive as soon as possible under the new male order, and thus cut her losses.

There is more than strife and tragedy in the lives of red howler females. These stressful incidents are only a small part of a howler's life. Yet, the outcomes of these events—maturity, possible emigration, and the potential invasion of one's troop by hostile males—have profound implications for the reproductive success of females. Some females will be lucky; they will breed in natal troops that never get invaded during their lifetime. Others will emigrate, waste part of their reproductive lives in extratroop existence, or find themselves in a newly formed troop that soon dissolves. Still others will be eaten before their time. This is a far cry from the picture of primate societies in decades past, when we imagined docile mothers did little more than raise cute infants. It's not the monkeys that have changed, but rather our perspective.

Update

Since my research on the red howlers of Venezuela ended in 1987, more evidence has emerged indicating that infanticide is a common occurrence among howlers (Crockett and Sekulic 1984; Crocket and Eisenberg 1987; Crockett 1997). At Hato Masaguaral between 1989 and 1991, researchers witnessed five more infanticides and reported eight suspicious infant disappearances after males invaded red howler troops. In Colombia, male invasions occurred in one red howler troop about every one-and-a-half years, and eight of twelve infants born were observed or suspected infanticide victims. Infanticides associated with new adult males entering troops with young infants have been reported for three more howler species, *Alouatta caraya* in Argentina, *A. fusca* in Brazil, and *A. pigra* in Belize.

The pattern of female emigration has continued at Hato Masaguaral (Crockett and Pope 1988, 1993). Theresa Pope and I found that the likelihood of dispersal by woodland and gallery forest females was directly related to the number of adult females already in their natal troops. All dispersal-age females left troops that already had four reproductive females. Young females were most likely to breed in natal troops with only one or two adult females. Emigrant females successfully breeding in newly formed troops were significantly older when they first gave birth, a median of 6.9 years versus 5.1 years for natal females. The dispersing females often ranged widely and encountered difficulties in joining a long-lasting new troop.

In 1984 I had speculated that the reason for red howler troops having no more than four adult females was related to food competetion, as troop size increases with the number of females (Crockett 1984). Howlers are known to be energy conservers and might not be able to travel an expansive home range to support the food needs of a larger troop. However, recently Charlie Janson and I have examined the data in a new way that suggests that a better explanation ties female emigration to infanticide risk (Crockett and janson 1993). In short, the likelihood of infanticide is greater in troops with more adult females, apparently because invading males are attracted to troops with more potential mates. Thus, females are better off in smaller troops. Young females might prefer to stay in their natural troops but are sometimes forced to leave, probably most often by unrelated females. Female-female competition still appears to be the main reason that red howler troops are small, but infanticide avoidance rather than food competition seems to be the evolutionary explanation.

References Cited

CROCKETT, C M. 1984. Emigration by female red howler monkeys and the case for female competition. In *Female Primates: Studies by Women Primatologists,* edited by M. F. Small, 159-173. New York: Alan R. Liss.

CROCKETT, C. M, AND R.SEKULIC. 1984. Infanticide in red howler monkeys *(Alouatta seniculus).* In *Infanticide: Comparative and Evolutionary Perspectives,* edited by G. Hausfater and S. B. Hrdy, 173-191. New York: Aldine.

CROCKETT, C.M., AND J. EISENBERG 1987. Howlers: Variations in group size and demography. In *Primate Societies,* edited by B. B. Smuts, D. L. Cheney, R. M. Seyfarth, R. W. Wrangham, and T. T. Struhsaker, 54-68. Chicago: University of Chicago Press.

CROCKET, C. M., AND C. H. JANSON. 1993. The costs of sociality in red howler monkeys: Infanticide or food competition? *American journal of Primatology* 30:306.

CROCKETT, C. M., AND T. R. POPE. 1988. Inferring patterns of aggression from red howler monkey injuries. *American journal of Primatology* 15:289-308.

CROCKETT, C. M., AND T. R. POPE. 1993. Consequences of sex differences in dispersal for juvenile red howler monkeys. In *Juvenile Primates: Life History, Development and Behavior,* edited by M. E. Pereira and L. A. Fairbanks, 104-118. New York; Oxford University Press.

CROCKETT, C M. 1996. The relation between red howler monkey troop size and population growth in two habitats. In *Adaptive Radiations of Neotropical Primates,* edited by M. Norconk, A. Rosenberger, and P. Garber, 489-510. New York: Plenum.

Aping Culture

By Meredith F. Small

Chimpanzees speak in dialects, invent odd grooming styles, and drum better than most kids in marching bands. So what's left to separate them from us?

In the summer of 1960, a young English woman stood on the shores of Lake Tanganyika looking into the hills of Gombe Stream Reserve with her mother. From the shore, Gombe seems impossible to negotiate: steep, tree-covered ridges and their corresponding ravines rise from the beach as if a giant child had reached down with spread fingers and scraped the landscape upward. The pant-hoot calls of chimpanzees—husky puffs of noise that rise quickly into wild screams—echo across the ravines and taunt any visitor to follow the apes across the undulating terrain.

The young woman spent the first months trying to catch up with her subjects, scrambling up cliffs, grabbing onto roots, and then standing perfectly still so as not to scare them away. The only way the chimps would tolerate her presence, she eventually found, was if she lured them close with bananas. Thus began a decades-long effort to follow around groups of chimpanzees to figure out what they can tell us about ourselves.

Her name, of course, was Jane Goodall, and in the years that followed she would become an icon of both sober science and exotic adventure. The willowy figure dressed in green fatigues, the limp blonde hair drawn back in a ponytail, the quiet British voice narrating innumerable National Geographic specials—these images and sounds are inextricably bound to the public's understanding of chimp behavior. Before Goodall's work, chimpanzees were known mostly from studies on animals that had been captured and imported to indoor and outdoor laboratories. Although psychobiologists like Robert Yerkes knew that chimps were smart, no one was sure how they used those smarts in the wild.

"When I went to Gombe, nothing was known," Goodall said recently, "Chimps weren't allowed to have personalities—no names, no reasoning ability, no emotions. Until one recognized the individuals, you couldn't work out the social structure, nor could you make any sense of the communication. It was so confusing." Goodall's work changed all that. Her detailed daily records of individual chimpanzees— maintained these days by other primatologists and field assistants—resulted in the first chimp personality portraits, as well as startling discoveries of chimpanzee tool use, hunting practices, and even murder.

That was just the beginning. For the past four decades, an army of researchers from Europe, Japan, and the United States has observed chimpanzees at more than 40 sites. In 1966 Toshisada Nishida began a study in the Mahale Mountains, 90 miles south of Gombe, and went on to identify the basic social structure of chimpanzee communities. In the 1970s, researchers discovered that chimps living in Guinea and Ivory Coast, on the far western edge of their species's range, hunted and used tools differently from their eastern cousins. A decade later, Richard Wrangham, working in both Gombe and the Kibale National Park in Uganda, showed that chimps can act much the same even when they live in different habitats and have different diets. Takayoshi Kano and others, meanwhile, have cast a new light on chimpanzee behavior through studies of the bonobo, the chimpanzee's more peaceable, more egalitarian cousin.

Last summer, researchers from seven long-term field sites combined their results in a landmark report in the journal *Nature*. Led by primatologist Andrew Whiten of the University of St. Andrews in Scotland, they listed 39 chimpanzee behaviors that go beyond mere survival strategies. More important, those behaviors vary from group to group: In some areas, for instance, chimpanzees dip for ants with a long stick, swipe the ants into a ball, and then flick the ball into their mouths. At other sites they use a short stick and slurp the ants with their tongues. Some chimpanzees dip the edges of leaves as a display; others use the leaves as napkins. Perusing the total list is a bit like thumbing through a Fodor's travel guide. And that is exactly the point. Chimpanzees, Whiten and his colleagues concluded, have culture.

Critics wasted no time in raising objections. Culture means more than just a set of learned behaviors that vary from place to place, some argued; culture means history and tradition, art, philosophy, and religion—the last barrier, together with language, that separates humans from other species. Others voiced more subtle concerns: "Are we measuring what we really think we are measuring?" anthropologist John Mitani of the University of Michigan wonders. "Just because it's different at two different places—is it culture?"

Jane Goodall

The debate boils down to semantics as much as science, and it largely misses the point. The fact that different chimps learn different ways to act hardly makes them human—it may not even make them cultural. But it does raise a far more intriguing question, one that has long seemed unanswerable: What can those learned behaviors tell us about the origins and purpose of human culture?

The Bossou Nature Reserve in the Republic of Guinea pops up from the West African plain like a green thumb. It looks almost out of place—a leafy oasis in a sea of humanity, a spot of nature amid peasant villages and irrigated rice and manioc farms But this forest was here long before the people began cutting down the trees, planting crops, and corralling the resident chimps toward their last stand. Today, a village sits at the base of the reserve, and villagers, looking up, can see the animals bounce among the trees. Their backyard is essentially a natural exhibit of chimpanzees.

And what curious chimps they are. As one walks up the hillside, out of the village and into the forest, the hubbub of talking, laughing, and shouting people fades away, and the air begins to ring with hollow knocks and smacks. It sounds as if workers in a factory are beating some product into shape, but a closer look shows that it's a group of chimpanzees sitting together cracking nuts. An old female grabs a heavy stone and makes sure it's flat, then wedges another stone underneath it to keep it from rocking. She places an oil palm nut on top, into a spot worn smooth from hours of smashing. Holding a lighter stone in her hand, she raises it high above her head and slams it down, crushing the nut to pieces. She then delicately picks out the nut meats and chews them contemplatively, clearly enjoying her fatty snack.

What makes this scene so interesting is not just that chimps are smart enough to figure out how to

Chimpanzees grooming each other at Gombe

crack hard-shelled nuts, but that their method of doing so is specific to West Africa. In the Mahale Mountains in East Africa, chimpanzees walk right by those nuts, oblivious to their nutritious meats. Moreover, nut-cracking is clearly a learned behavior, since it takes years to master. When young chimps at Bossou try their hand at it, primatologist Tetsuro Matsuzawa has found, the nuts keep slipping off the flat stone, or the young chimps can't hit them, or they strike at a bad angle and the nut goes whizzing through the forest like an errant bullet. It takes years of watching how it's done, and lots of practice, before the youngsters get anywhere.

Nut-cracking has all the elements of a cultural behavior: It only occurs at some sites and is passed down by learning and imitation. But other presumed cultural differences are more subtle. For example, John Mitani has found that male chimpanzees' pant-hoots crescendo differently depending on where they live At one site, the calls sound like a train slowly leaving the station—chug-ah, chug-ah, chug-ah—gradually accelerating toward a scream. Elsewhere the buildup is faster, higher-pitched, and more frantic. More intriguing still, males at each site seem to modulate their voices so that their calls sound alike. By doing so, they are presumably announcing their joint presence and confirming that they belong to the same group.

Mitani tentatively calls these different pant-hoots "dialects," but he acknowledges that what he hears may be a product of differences in body size, genes, or habitat. "It wouldn't be fair to compare the calls produced by West African chimps, who are larger and have deeper voices, with small East African chimps," he explains. Yet the calls don't seem to be tailored to their habitats either. In the Mahale Mountains, low-pitched calls would carry farthest, yet the chimps have relatively high voices; in Gombe's open woodland, high-pitched calls would travel best, but the chimps have low voices.

Even if the differences in calls are learned, some linguists might question Mitani's terms. When he says that chimpanzees have dialects, he means that different groups make different sounds even though their members can intermingle. But when people are said to speak a dialect, the term means more than just distinctive sounds. "Dialects are two versions of a language that are still mutually comprehensible," says Robbins Burling, a linguist at the University of Michigan. Or as Massachusetts Institute of Technology psychologist Steven Pinker puts it: "The standard definition is that a language is a dialect with an army and a navy." Pinker is quick to add that Mitani's use of the term is "innocuous." But even the most open-minded linguist or primatologist wouldn't say that chimpanzees speak a language.

Does it matter? Do chimpanzees have to be so much like humans to have culture? The answer depends on your definition of culture—and a dozen anthropologists will give you a dozen different definitions. If, as some say, culture is any learned behavior that is shared by a collective, chimpanzees easily make the grade. As Barbara Miller, a cultural anthropologist at the George Washington University, puts it: "If we take a broader approach to culture, as I do, and include foraging behavior and sex, much of what chimpanzees do would be considered culture " But other anthropologists are more discriminating. Culture, they argue, is what people say and think, not what they do; it deals with symbols and meaning rather than behavior. Practicing a religion is cultural, according to this definition; plowing a field is not.

If that's the case, chimpanzees will never join the culture club. "None of us," anthropologist William McGrew admits, "knows what significance chimpanzees attach to some of the weird and wonderful things they do." Still, Whiten and his colleagues have shown that chimps can imitate complex behaviors step by step (though they never teach one another deliberately). The longer primatologists study chimpanzees and the more their findings are compared, the longer the list of unique learned behaviors grows.

Taken together, those traits may open a window on early human behavior as well. For example, according to a recent survey of five long-term chimp studies, the most sociable chimps tend to be best at using tools (captive chimps, by the same token, are better with tools than wild chimps). That pattern may help explain how early hominids, despite their smaller brains, gradually developed complex cultures. After all, fossil evidence shows that early humans only began to use tools after their canines (which they may have used to fight one another) began to shrink.

To get a less theoretical sense of how chimp culture and human culture are related, you might try standing quietly in Kibale National Park and listening hard. Chances are, instead of the monotonous sound of nut-cracking, you'll hear something more complex: a hollow knocking, a double-time thump-thumping that echoes through the trees.

Chimpanzees, You'll Find, Can Drum

The trees at Kibale and other sites often have huge buttresses that rise several yards from the leafy litter to the canopy overhead. By slapping at the buttresses with their hands, chimps can create rhythmic patterns that can carry for more than a mile. Adam Clark Arcadi, an anthropologist at Cornell University, has spent four years collecting these sounds. To do so, he and his research assistants simply stand in the forest and point a directional microphone toward a drummer. Later, back in his lab. Arcadi runs the recording through a sophisticated computer program that creates images of the sound, From that image he can measure differences in rhythm and pitch among drummers.

Chimp drumming is a male thing, as far as we know. Males do it throughout the day, most often when on the move, with each bout lasting anywhere from a few seconds to almost half a minute. Like jazz drummers knocking out a riff, each chimp seems to have a signature beat. "There are differences in the speed at which they drum, and in slaps that come in pairs—ba-dump-ba-dump-ba-dump—versus single beats—dump-dump-dump," Arcadi explained one day, hitting his desk to demonstrate. Like people, chimps can be righties or lefties, and they probably favor their better hand when drumming. When Arcadi played some of his drumming tapes, spliced together into a continuous loop, it sounded like elementary jazz.

All chimpanzees presumably drum to communicate with one another (though no one knows what they're communicating). But Arcadi has found that males at Kibale often drum without calling, whereas males in Tai National Park usually pant-hoot as well. One could say. therefore, that chimpanzee drumming is multicultural. Maybe there's even a link between what chimps pound out in the forest and the sounds that their human counterparts make on a Saturday night.

To deepen our concept of their culture, primatologists will have to learn more about chimps' interpersonal relationships. Do chimps from various sites treat each other differently? Are the customs and manners of East African chimps as different from those of West African chimps as, say, Samoans' are from Icelanders'? Are males more repressive toward females at one site and more easygoing at another, echoing the variety of human male-female relationships across the globe? In the words of primatologist Frans B.M. de Waal, who observes chimpanzee social behavior at the Yerkes Primate Field Station in Atlanta: "Who fishes for ants and who doesn't, or who cracks nuts and who doesn't—that's the easy thing to see. But the social dynamics, that's much harder to put your finger on."

Who knows what's left to discover? "I now regard chimpanzees as a very big mystery," says anthropologist Vernon Reynolds, who works in Uganda's Budongo Forest. "The more we find out, the less we understand." McGrew agrees: "I have been struck by the richness of chimpanzee nature. There is always a new twist on an old theme that causes you to smile and revise yet another set of conclusions. There is such a wonderful wealth of stuff here."

Late in the fall, Jane Goodall took some time away from her most recent book tour—and plans for yet another African safari—to talk about the chimp culture studies. The new findings hardly come as a surprise, she said. "I wrote an article in 1973 saying that the big challenge now, the most important thing, is to learn about cultural variation." As for the definition of culture, she still uses the one she has always used: "It's simple. You just have to prove that the behavior is passed down through observational learning rather than instinct."

Nevertheless, the studies that Goodall set in motion so long ago are quickly carrying us beyond such simple answers. Perhaps chimpanzees are more guided by cultural rules in their day-to-day interactions than we realize. Or perhaps some of the activities that we consider patently cultural—in humans as well as chimps—are really shaped by the environment.

"I don't think everything humans do is cultural," says cultural anthropologist Lee Cronk of Rutgers University. In one Kenyan tribe, for instance, tradition dictates that boys are more desirable than girls, yet parents consistently treat girls better. The reason, Cronk says, is that girls in that area are more likely than boys to give their parents grandchildren. Culture may urge one behavior, but biology urges another—and the latter wins out.

"Culture isn't what we do," Cronk concludes, "it's the information that we share that tells us what's appropriate to do. It's not the act of baking a cake; it's the recipe." The trick is determining when we're improvising and when we're cooking by the book. What part of marriage, for instance, is biological and what part cultural? "Culture is complicated when it comes to humans," Cronk admits. "But with chimps it's relatively simple. You can get your mind around it. It allows you to see very clearly that they behave in many ways with no cultural input. When people see that, it's easier to convince them that, yeah, culture isn't the only thing that is influencing human behavior."

Goodall's definition of culture, cut-and-dried as it sounds, still smudges such distinctions For decades she has been the preeminent authority on chimpanzees, and her major work, The Chimpanzees of Gombe, has been a kind of bible to primatologists. Published in 1986, its 673 pages once seemed to contain everything one could ever want to know about chimps. These days, though, when you get it down from the bookshelf, you notice that the pages have yellowed, and that a damp, musty library smell rises from them. The Chimpanzees of Gombe no longer seems a sacred text, but a piece of history.

And soon, it may be a relic.

Married to the Mob

By Sharon Gursky-Doyen

Brave in the face of predators and flexible in their family arrangements, tarsiers offer clues to the origins of sociality in primates.

It may be two o' clock in the morning, but that's the middle of the workday when you are monitoring a nocturnal animal. I am on a mountainside in Tangkoko Nature Reserve on the Indonesian island of Sulawesi, using a flashlight and radio-tracking device to keep tabs on a diminutive primate, a spectral tarsier (Tarsius spectrum). All of a sudden I hear high-pitched shrieks from higher up the mountain. Following those sounds, I pick my way up the steep, forested slope as fast as I can. Somewhere a group of tarsiers is upset, and I want to know why. As I get closer to the commotion, I slow down, not knowing what awaits me. Cautiously, I scan the foliage for tarsiers and for whatever threat has caused them to call with such urgency. Then I see it: a large python coiled up in a tight ball. Four, five, no, six spectral tarsiers—each no bigger than my hand—are sounding the alarm. And they are all leaping toward the python.

The tiny tarsiers repeatedly lunge so close to the intruder that I think they are about to become snake dinner, and then they leap out of reach. One individual is truly brazen: he jumps onto the python's back and bites it! The snake's muscles ripple as it tries to capture and strangle the animal on its back. But the daring tarsier is too quick, and darts away. For nearly thirty minutes, the tarsiers lunge and retreat; even the individual I was following earlier arrives to join in the mobbing. Finally the python uncurls—it must be twelve feet long—and slithers away. After calling for another twenty minutes the tarsiers move off. But they remain skittish throughout the night, breaking out into alarm calls and frequently returning to the scene of the face-off.

The spectral tarsiers mobbing of a predator is a total surprise. What might have prompted such brazen—and coordinated—behavior? I know that a male female pair and two offspring, a juvenile female and an infant, sleep during the day near the site of the incident. But on my nightly "focal follows," the excursions in which I track the activity of one individual, I rarely encounter more than one or two tarsiers in any one place. Yet I've just seen at least six adults join together In attacking a python. Maybe the species is more gregarious than anyone has realized. And the incident is significant in another way: the vast majority of species known to mob predators are diurnal, not nocturnal.

Mobbing is but one of the enigmas about spectral tarsiers that have captured my attention over the past two decades. Another puzzle is why some individuals choose to be monogamous and others polygynous (one male mating with several females). Few species have such a variable mating system. By exploring those and other tarsier behavioral traits, and the ecological and social factors at play, I hope to shine a light on how group living evolved in primates.

dispute. The eighteenth-century French naturalist Button, who, upon examining a juvenile tarsier, thought it might be a kind of opossum, was not the first to find them a bundle of contradictions. While other living primates fall fairly neatly into two main groups—the Strepsirrhini (the suborder that embraces lemurs, lorises, and galagos) and the Haplorrhini (the one that includes monkeys, apes, and humans)—tarsiers seem to belong to both at once.

A variety of characteristics mark tarsiers as Strepsirrhini: their small body size, grooming claws, nocturnal habits, and two-horned (as opposed to single-chambered) uterus, as well as aspects of their parental care (a mother will park her infant in a tree while she forages, and infants are transported by mouth, the way a dog carries a). On the other hand tarsiers possess numerous features linking them with the Haplorrhini, including a dry nose, a mobile upper lip that is not attached to the nose, a fovea centralis (a depression in the middle of the retina that increases visual acuity), and a hemochoriai placenta, which provides dose contact between the mother's blood and the fetal circulatory system. Certain skeletal traits, most notably an eye socket backed by bone, also seem to favor a haplorrhine connection, but they may have evolved independently.

Most taxonomists today assign tarsiers to their own infraorder within the suborder Haplorrhini, but their unusual combination of traits shows that their lineage branched off long ago from the rest of the suborder. Fossils representing Tarsius and closely related genera, found in North America, Africa, and Asia, date as far back as 45 million years,

To begin with, they are extreme leapers. Indeed, they are named for an unusually long tarsal (ankle) bone that acts as their launcher. They are reportedly capable of leaping as far as eighteen feet; as a result, they can travel through the forest a lot faster than I can.

Then, tarsiers have the owl-like ability—shared with no other mammal—to rotate their heads backward 180 degrees. Often when I am out in the jungle tracking a tarsier, it will look in one direction, but then leap the opposite way! That makes it very easy to lose the individual I am following. And unlike the majority of nocturnal mammals—but like all haplorrhines—tarsiers lack the light-reflecting layer of tissue behind the retina known as the tapetum lucidum. In low light, that "bright carpet" improves vision and, as a byproduct, renders an animal's pupils visible as "eyeshine." Absent any eyeshine, the strikingly large eyes of tarsiers do not broadcast their location as one might hope.

When I first began studying tarsiers in the 1990s, they were considered solitary creatures, like most other nocturnal foragers. But when I started tracking them using radio telemetry, I learned that sometimes other tarsiers were not so far away. The conventional approach is to put a radio collar on an individual and track it over the course of one night, picking different nights to watch different individuals. To determine whether tarsiers might be more social than they were reputed to be, I tried a new technique. I would radio-collar a pair of tarsiers and perform "simultaneous focal follows" with an assistant: the two of us would synchronize our watches, each take a radio receiver, and then note our respective tarsier's location every five minutes over the course of twelve hours. So, for example, I might observe a mother while my assistant would simultaneously track her offspring; or we might track two mates this way. Then we would compare our notes.

Once we started watching pairs rather than individuate, we discovered that spectral tarsiers are far from solitary. A majority of the sexually mature adults are monogamous, and mates often stay together for most of their lives, which average seven years: With their immature offspring (as many as two per female) they occupy home territories in small family groups. Although direct paternal care is rare, if is common for a member of the group other than the mother-typically an adolescent sister of the infant-to help with the caretaking. Examples of such "allomothering" include sharing food, babysitting, grooming, and playing. An adolescent female will also transport a young infant by mouth if, say, it falls out of a tree where the mother parked it.

Spectral tarsiers are territorial. They use their urine and various body glands to scent-mark along the boundaries of their home range; they announce their claim with early-morning family choruses, and they vocally confront and chase any members of neighboring groups that threaten to intrude. They exhibit tremendous attachment to a particular site, with individuals and sometimes family groups continually using the same sleeping tree for years.

How might those patterns of behavior have evolved? When I surveyed the primate literature, I found that three main factors had been hypothesized to lead to sociality, or gregariousness, in primates. One is infanticide: if outsiders of their own species pose a threat, relatives stick together to defend their offspring. Another is food abundance: the patchier the distribution of food in the habitat, the more a group may need to come together to share and defend their resources. And finally there is predation pressure; members of a group cooperate to warn and defend against common enemies.

Infanticide has been observed in captive tarsiers, but does infanticide—or the threat of it—play a role in wild tarsier sociality? I kept track of how much time males spent near females, noting whether or not the females were pregnant or lactating. When a female was lactating—that is, had an infant—the average distance between the male and female of a pair was significantly less than when the female was pregnant or at some other point in her cycle: 85 feet versus 135 feet. By remaining near and traveling with the female and the new infant, her mate could prevent neighboring males from getting too close and killing the infant.

Given the exceptionally large prenatal investment tarsier females must make, it is not surprising that males must help protect the infant. Newborn infants weigh about a third of the mother's weight—imagine a 120-pound woman producing a 40-pound baby! However, the presence of an infant only explained a small proportion of the gregariousness exhibited by spectral tarsiers, since the majority of social interactions did not involve infants.

I therefore began examining the role of food abundance. To record insect distribution on the ground and in the air, I began collecting insects by means of pitfall traps (holes in the ground), sweep nets (similar to butterfly nets), and Malaise traps (stationary nets named for the Swedish entomologist Rene Malaise). I found that individual tarsiers were more likely to remain near other group members when insect abundance was high rather than low: the average distance between group members was 87 feet compared with 175 feet.

Although the level of sociality was increased by food availability, as it was by the presence of an infant, it did not even come close to the coordinated mobbing behavior that I had observed during the python incident. Obviously, I needed to explore the effect of predators.

As you might imagine, interactions between tarsiers and their predators are relatively rare and difficult to observe. I thus looked for ways to mimic the presence of predators. First, I used physical models of predators, such as carved wooden civets, rubber snakes, and plastic birds of prey: and second. I recorded the vocalizations of predators at zoos and then played them back in tarsier territory.

In 74 percent of encounters with a robber python, the tarsiers alarm-called, and in 42 percent of the incidents, once joined by other individuals, they also mobbed the snake. Such an encounter had a back, the tarsiers responded in 42 percent of the experiments by alarm-calling, and in 38 percent by both alarm-calling and mobbing the speakers.

The model civet often elicited harsh alarm calls, but it was mobbed in only about 10 percent of the encounters. Thinking the experimental setup might be overlooking the tarsiers' well-developed sense of smell I organized a new set of tests, I observed the reactions of twenty different adults as each was exposed to four different situations: a wooden civet model covered in civet urine, a wooden civet without urine. a stick covered in civet urine, and a stick without urine.

The results were revealing. The tarsiers never ignored the wooden model with civet urine: it provoked alarm calling every time, and they mobbed it in 77 percent of the encounters. In contrast, when exposed to the wooden civet model without urine, the tarsiers responded with alarm calls 39 percent of the time and with both alarm calls and mobbing 15 percent of the time; during 48 percent of the trials, they ignored it. In response to the stick with urine, the tarsiers alarm-called during 93 percent of the trials, but never mobbed; they ignored it in 7 percent of the trials. Unsurprisingly, the stick without urine provoked no response at all.

Mobbing is obviously a risky tactic, yet in both sets of experiments, more adult tarsiers mobbed the ostensible predator than resided in the local territory. What drove other adults to get involved? I observed that adult females regularly attended mobbings, but they were usually passive participants, alarm-calling nearby and watching from a safe distance. The aggressive participants, those lunging at

exchanges. That hypothesis predicts that mobbing will be restricted to groups with young infants. However, I found that mobbing occurred just as often in groups without immature offspring, thus knocking a hole in that explanation. Another idea is that mobbing instills "site avoidance." That is, individuals will avoid a locale where a predator was previously encountered and mobbed. But tarsier mothers apparently had no qualms about parking an infant in or near a tree where they were previously exposed to a rubber snake. The data did not support that hypothesis.

According to the "perception advertisement" hypothesis, the potential prey animals, by openly identifying themselves (in this case through mobbing), inform the predator that it has lost the advantage of surprise. Discouraged, the predator then leaves. Naturally, the opportunity to test that was limited to when an actual snake appeared. But based on preliminary observations, the hypothesis fell flat: there was little evidence that the snake spent significantly less time in the area after being mobbed than when the tarsiers only emitted alarm calls or just ignored it. The same set of observations also rejected the "move-on" hypothesis, which states that because it is discomforted by harassment, a predator entering an area will leave sooner the more intensely it is mobbed.

Finally, the "cultural transmission" hypothesis states that an individual learns to fear an object when it witnesses other animals mobbing it, and thus learns to avoid it or mob It in the future. However, when studying the response of infants, I found that nursing infants, even in their first week of life, alarm-called when exposed to a model snake, despite never having seen a snake previously. Their awareness of danger from snakes was not culturally transmitted, undermining that hypothesis.

Because none of the above hypotheses seemed satisfactory, I proposed a new one spectral tarsiers mob predators as a "costly signal." In effect, the signaler advertises that it can afford to perform an otherwise detrimental act-something that a weaker competitor cannot do as effectively. The classic costly signal is the peacock's tail. The tail makes the bird more vulnerable to predators, but the message to the potential mate is, "I have survived in spite of this huge tail, hence I am fitter." Similarly, while aggregating around a dangerous snake, tarsier males may demonstrate their current physical condition, agility, and speed-and therefore suitability as a mate. According to this hypothesis, the trait of mobbing behavior has evolved in males because it is attractive to females, thus increasing a male's chances of procreating. The driving force is a type of natural selection known as sexual selection.

Because spectral tarsier groups contain only one adult male, any additional males that show up at a "mob scene" must come from other groups. But I observed that males did not show up at all such events. In 80 percent of the cases, including both experimentally elicited and naturally occurring events, males preferred to join groups that contained adolescent females-they came to impress the gals! By observing the males mobbing, young females can evaluate the ability and willingness of males to protect them and their future offspring against predators

Mobbing, then, seems to be a way for a male to get an adolescent female to leave her group and form a new pair. That conclusion naturally made me curious about why tarsiers join groups, leave groups, or remain in their parental group. To this end, I started to explore dispersal—the permanent departure of an animal from its original home.

Because dispersal involves leaving the protection of a familiar group and territory, an animal that takes the plunge increases its risk of predation and takes a gamble on finding food resources. Therefore the payoff needs to be significant. In mammals, males tend to be the ones to seek new territories. One of the most widely accepted explanations for that is the preponderance of polygynous mating systems-one male siring the offspring of several females in a group, in a polygynous group, the females invest more time and energy in their offspring than the male does. Consequently, they usually have a greater stake in a home range proven to have sufficient resources for successful reproduction, and the mates are the ones likely to strike out on their own.

Starting in 1994 and continuing through 2008, I tracked seventy-four banded individuals, noting their location relative to their initial sleeping trees. Both sexes proved equally likely to disperse from their natal territories, but males dispersed significantly farther than females, an average of 2,165 feet away, compared with 873 feet for females. One possible explanation for the difference in distance may be that it reduces the chances of inbreeding.

Like many territorial primates, spectral tarsiers return to the same tree when it is time to sleep. They prefer hollowed-out fig trees with multiple entrances and exits. These typically form when a "strangler" fig tree grows around another tree, kills it, and the dead supporting tree rots away, leaving an empty space. In measuring the diameters (at "breast height," 4.5 feet aboveground) and heights of their sleeping trees, I was able to demonstrate that individuals residing in larger sleeping trees were more likely to be found at the same site in later years, while individuals residing in smaller frees were more likely to move, I also discovered that polygynous groups were more likely to have the larger sleeping trees.

While there are a few primate species that vary in their mating patterns, rarely has the variation been observed within a single population, such as that inhabiting the Tangkoko Nature Reserve. Consequently, I wanted to know what led individual tarsiers to choose monogamy or, much less frequently (about 15 percent of the time), polygyny. In some species, the male's help is required in order to successfully rear offspring, and that favors what Devra G. Kleiman, an ethologist and conservation biologist affiliated with the Smithsonian National groups, we were able to conclude that polygyny is not limited by insect biomass, insect abundance, or territory size, but primarily by access to high-quality sleeping sites—that is, tall, wide fig trees. Real estate ruled!

Groups that were fortunate enough to possess territories with large fig trees for sleeping sites were significantly more likely to be polygynous than were groups whose sleeping trees were smaller or of another species. While monogamous groups consistently used only one sleeping site, polygynous groups tended to have multiple sites, giving them more options if something were to happen to one of their sleeping trees. That is a significant issue, because tree falls are frequent, owing to the high winds at Tangkoko Nature Reserve and the diffuse root structure of the fig trees. Although fig trees are fairly common within the reserve, those making the best sleeping sites are relatively rare, which is why polygyny is so much less common than monogamy.

In choosing a mate, a female spectral tarsier apparently looks not only for a male whose mobbing displays demonstrate his readiness to defend her and her offspring against predators, but also, where possible, for one whose territory includes at least one high-quality sleeping site. Why would such a

their ancestors and other early primates responded to predators. Snakes are persistent predators of modern placental mammals, and according to Lynne Isbell, an anthropologist at the University of California, Davis, they may have been major driving forces of evolutionary change in mammals. Their ability to hunt, moving silently even in the trees, was and remains a major threat to primates. Mobbing behavior may have evolved as a survival tactic in the face of that threat and, in turn, been a major leap toward group living.

Sharon Gursky-Doyen is an associate professor of anthropology at Texas A&M University. She received her PhD from the State University of new York at Stony Brook and has been studying tarslers throughout Sulawesi, Indonesia, since 1990. While continuing her work on spectral tarsiers, she is also investigating the effects of altitude on the recently redis-covered pygmy tarsier (Tarsius pumilus). She is the author of The Spectral Tarsier (Prentice Hail, 2007) and coeditor (with K.A.I. Nekaris) of Primate Anti-Predator Strategies (Springer, 2007).

Dance of the Sexes

By Sharon T. Pochron and Patricia C. Wright

A lemur needs some unusual traits to survive in Madagascar's unpredictable environment.

The group of lemurs, known as Milne-Edwards's sifakas, was small—an adult male, an adult female, and two large offspring. With only four animals, distinguishing them should have been easy. "That's the male," said Georges Rakotonirina, pointing. Rakotonirina was the lead field technician, a native of Madagascar who had been studying the sifakas with one of us (Wright) since 1988. "And that's the female." The novice among us (Pochron), new to the study in 2000, stared at the dark forms up in the tree and blinked. They all looked the same.

"Look," said Rakotonirina. "They're eating vahiabanikondro."

"What?" Pochron thought to herself. "How can he tell from down here what they're eating? And can I possibly learn to pronounce and spell ... whatever it is?" Hearing chattering in the forest canopy, Pochron then asked aloud, "What bird is that?"

Rakotonirina laughed. "That's the sifaka," he said. "It means he wants to stop fighting." Pochron knew then and there she had some catching up to do, notwithstanding her previous experience studying baboons in Tanzania. But like Wright and many others whose first encounter with lemurs was life-changing, she was hooked.

The lemurs of Madagascar are the surviving members of a lineage that has been genetically isolated from the rest of the primate family for at least 65 million years. The island became separated from the African mainland 160 million years ago and from the Indian landmass 80 million years ago. The ancestors of lemurs probably colonized the island by rafting there on drifting vegetation. Until relatively recently, lemurs rived In a separate world. Meanwhile, primates elsewhere evolved into monkeys, apes, and humans.

That ancient genetic split is surely one reason lemurs often boast such unusual traits, compared with humanity's closer primate relatives. For example, dwarf lemurs store up fat In their tails and then draw on it while hibernating; in contrast, no monkey or ape hibernates. Members of one lemur family, the indrilds, maintain an upright, kangaroo-like posture as they leap from one tree trunk and cling to another; monkeys, however, are quadrupedal, like squirrels. All lemurs have toothcombs—a set of teeth ideally shaped for grooming; monkey and ape teeth are shaped for biting and chewing.

Especially surprising to evolutionary biologists, in most groups of lemurs, females are dominant over males, in some lemur species female dominance becomes manifest only in conflicts over food; in other species it emerges In all social settings. Yet in monkeys and apes—indeed, in mammals generally—female dominance is rare. What has led to such an unusual social characteristic among lemurs, with its far-reaching implications?

Sharon T. Pochron and Patricia C. Wright, "Dance of the Sexes," from *Natural History*, vol. 114, no. 5; June 2005 , pp. 34-39.

similar, when it comes to physical strength. How do females manage to get their way without the brawn to back up a threat? We and our colleagues do not yet have a definitive answer to that question, but after eighteen years studying one indriid species, we have some inklings.

The center of our universe is the Milne-Edwards's sifaka (Propithecus edwardsi). Until recently it was considered a subspecies of the diademed sifaka, but geneticists have now determined that it is a separate species. Weighing in at about thirteen pounds and looking like something out of the Muppet studio, the animal lives throughout Ranomafana National Park, a 170-square-mile emerald forest set in cloud-covered mountains, and in adjacent regions [see map on preceding page]. It has orange eyes and woolly, water-resistant fur (a useful trait in a rainforest) which is colored dark brown to black except for two large, white patches on the animal's back. The females have a lemony, maple-syrupy smell; the males, which have more glands for scent marking, smell muskier.

Active by day, Milne-Edwards's sifakas prefer to hang out some forty feet up in the trees, and they travel, as do other indrilds, by leaping from one tree trunk to the next. Adults are mainly leaf eaters, but they also rely heavily on fruits and seeds.

Females and males do not often come into conflict, but when they do, the females win about 95 percent of the time. Apparently males are letting females win such altercations. What are they giving up by submitting? The answer may be calories. Adult females, for instance, appear to eat more seeds than adult males do. The difference is most pronounced during the mating season. Seeds are generally high

having. If he allows a female to take his food, and she uses it to raise another male's offspring, he has not helped himself at all. So why would he allow her to win extra calories? Nature is hardly known for its generosity. In our years of field observations seeking answers to this question, we have found ourselves bumping into some other unusual and fascinating lemur traits. Our goal, then, is to find a coherent explanation that makes sense of it all: with apologies to the high-energy physicists, our holy grail is a kind of grand unified theory of the lemur.

Milne-Edwards's sifakas usually occur in small groups ranging from two to nine individuals. Typically, the groups include three adults (either two males and one female, or vice versa), infants, and older offspring. A female may come into her brief period of estrus at any time during the mating season, which runs from late November through mid-January. The babies are born in May, June, and July. A female gives birth to only one baby at a time, and nurses it attentively until the next mating season, if it survives until then. The cycle puts weaning at a propitious time, when food is most likely to be abundant. A mother that has nursed a baby that long is apt to skip a year before breeding again, most likely because it takes a while to store up enough fat.

Within a group of sifakas life is reasonably peaceful: members spend a lot more time grooming each other than they do squabbling. Males within a group get along most of the year. During the mating season, though, fights between mates can be among the most aggressive in this species. There is little question that the fights are about sex, and the fact that fighters sometimes suffer injuries to their testicles may be no accident. You can tell that a threatening look, a swipe, or a bite has had an effect if you hear the intended target emit birdlike chatter, the equivalent of, "Stop picking on me! I'll leave now!"

Since the males are clearly competing with each other for access to fertile females, it is puzzling that mates have not evolved to be larger than the females (or to have bigger teeth or other such endowments). According to classic behavioral ecology, when males compete, the larger or stronger males usually prevail. The larger males thus have more offspring, and those offspring carry the genes associated with being large. After several generations the repeated selection for large males should lead to males that are larger than the females. When the males and females of a species differ in such physical characteristics, the species is said to be sexually dimorphic.

Most large mammal species are sexually dimorphic. Monomorphism, where it is found, typically occurs in monogamous species, in which a single male and female pair up to raise their offspring together. To succeed evolutionarily, monogamy has to be a two-way street. The male has the genetic incentive to help feed, carry, and protect the young of a particular female only if the monogamous bond assures him the young are his. If the female needs a devoted mate to help raise her young, she has a genetic incentive of her own-to avoid mating with a male that beats up other males, because, despite winning the "right" to take many "wives," he cannot offer parental care to all his offspring. When male fighting is suppressed by such female preferences, so too is sexual dimorphism. Some lemurs such as indris (Indri indri) fit that pattern: they are monomorphic and monogamous [for a comparison of the indri with the diademed sifaka, see "Scent Wars," by Joyce A. Powzyk, April 2002].

Paradoxically, though, most lemur species do not behave like this in that they mate promiscuously, and males provide little or no care for infants, which may or may not be theirs. In short, they look like monogamous species, but they act like nonmonogamous ones. The Milne-Edwards's sifaka fits that pattern, too. But how can it be a stable arrangement?

Our observations offer part of the solution to the puzzle. First, no male, even if he is stronger than other males, can prevent a female from mating promiscuously. Nor does a larger male have the advantage of producing more sperm, because during the breeding season the testicles of all the males are roughly the same size. Thus the ejaculate of a heavy male cannot, as has been observed in some mammalian and avian species, overwhelm the ejaculate of a light mate: if they both mate with a particular female, each has an equal chance to father her offspring.

Aside from the competition between males over females, serious fighting may also erupt when a new adult animal joins a group. Such transitions in group membership shed additional light on the roles of males and females—and, in particular, the dominance of females—within lemur groups.

Milne-Edwards's sifaka groups are far less predictable in composition than those of monkey and ape species. A baboon troop, for instance, characteristically includes many adult males and females. Gorilla groups are generally polygynous, consisting of one silverback male, his harem of several adult females, their young, and one or more subordinate males. By contrast, sifaka groups can be polyandrous (one female and two or more males) or polygynous (one male and two or more females). They can include multiple males and multiple females-or just one adult pair [see illustration on page 36].

Not only do all such combinations turn up with roughly equal frequency, but a group may change in composition from one year to the next. A new member is most likely to join a group from August until October, just before the mating season. If a new male seeks to join a group, all the animals may coexist peacefully. Sometimes, though, the resident male and the newcomer fight, and one is driven away. And sometimes a female prefers the new male, and she may help force the old male to leave.

For any dependent offspring in the group, an incoming male poses great danger: he is likely to kill them, a measure that is evolutionarily adaptive because it speeds up his chance to father offspring. Such behavior is well documented in primates.

When an adult female tries to join a group, friction with the resident female seems inevitable. The two sometimes bite, slap, and chase each other. The

To investigate why the sifaka's social arrangements vary so widely, we compared sifaka survivorship and fertility patterns with those of some other primates. For example, tamarins and marmosets, both New World monkeys, suffer high mortality in their early years; sensibly, then, they reach sexual maturity and begin reproducing at an early age. By contrast, many Old World monkeys, such as baboons and macaques, live longer, start to reproduce later, and have more time between babies.

The mortality pattern of the Milne-Edwards's sifaka closely resembles that of the tamarins and marmosets: many die in their first few years of life. In fertility, however, Milne-Edwards's sifakas resemble baboons and macaques: the sifakas that do survive reach sexual maturity fairly late (about three and a half years for females, and four and a half years for males), and they reproduce at a slow rate over a span approaching thirty years. It is almost as if sifakas have deliberately chosen the most difficult of all the primate patterns ever observed: high mortality coupled with slow reproduction. By the end of her life, a female tamarin or marmoset will have three or four daughters; a baboon or macaque will have two or three. But by the end of her lifespan, a female sifaka will rarely have more than one daughter that survives to reproduce. The constraints on reproduction may be responsible for encouraging the sifakas' highly flexible group structures.

The sifaka's lifespan is unusual for a mammal its size. On average, the larger the species, the longer It lives. As we noted earlier, Milne-Edwards's sifakas weigh about thirteen pounds, yet they live nearly thirty years in the wild. Such longevity may have original question about lemurs: why are females the dominant sex? The behavioral pattern, in which males cede food to females, appears essential for balancing female and male reproductive needs. For females, fertility, pregnancy., and nursing all depend on sufficient body weight. Weight is less important for males, because their reproductive role Is limited to copulation and, as we mentioned earlier, during the breeding season, the testes of small-bodied males are the same size as those of larger-bodied males. If the males did grow larger overall. Madagascar's unpredictable environment might prove fatal to them. In sum, neither having a small body size nor relinquishing high-calorie foods to females seems to compromise the fertility of males.

In the past few years we have considered a number of ways to account for these observations. Because the females mate promiscuously, perhaps each male simply defers to all females, on the grounds that there is always some chance that one of them will bear his offspring. Or a male may yield food to a female only when he has some good reasons for thinking he will sire her offspring. Or a male may defer to a close female relative (mother, sister, daughter), whose offspring would indirectly share some of his genes. Or maybe the reality is some combination of all those factors [see illustration on page 37].

One way to learn more about what is going on is to test offspring for paternity. Toni Lyn Morelli, one of Wrights graduate students, has been sampling blood of these sifakas and analyzing it genetically. In a species where the average number of adults in a group is three, however, discerning a statistically significant pattern may take some time. And—who knows?—the results may lead us to some new lemur mystery.

Chapter 4

Human Evolution

Anthropology is the study of humans, so it should come as no surprise that the evolution of humans is a primary focus for many physical anthropologists. We humans have always been fascinated with ourselves, and the story of our origins can grasp the imagination in a way that few other scientific endeavors can match. Every fossil discovery has the potential to both answer questions and uncover new ones, to put some controversies to rest, or suggest fresh and intriguing possibilities. No other discipline within anthropology can change as much—or as quickly—as human evolutionary studies. We are always just one new fossil away from a potentially radically different understanding of our beginnings.

Of course, critics of evolution make a lot of noise about the many unknowns faced by paleoanthropologists (a paleoanthropologist is someone who studies the human fossil record). Most significantly, creationists claim that any arguments among scientists illuminate weaknesses in evolution itself. It is important to remember that science can only progress through study and debate. We are constantly learning new things by questioning old ideas and scrutinizing new data. Disagreements among scientists over details in the fossil record do not question

evolution itself, but instead seek better explanations for how those evolutionary changes occurred. As discussed in some of the articles in Section 1 of this book, the theory of evolution by natural selection is a well-established and strong scientific theory that is reinforced by these debates, which improve our understanding of how evolution proceeds.

The selection of articles in this section highlights some recent discoveries in paleoanthropology, and also discusses some of the current debates in the field. In "The Birth of Bipedalism," James Shreeve analyzes the implications of the recent publications describing a trove of *Ardipithecus ramidus* fossils, dating to over five million years ago. "The Downside of Upright" details how the development of bipedality in humans has led to a series of compromises in other necessary activities, like childbirth. In "New Find," you will read about a series of new fossils from the site of Dmanisi, which has forced paleoanthropologists to reevaluate our assumptions about the earliest hominids to leave Africa. The chapter wraps up with "Brothers in Arms," which discusses a murder mystery that is tens of thousands of years old. Each of these articles provides a glimpse into the dynamic science of human origins and evolution.

The Birth of Bipedalism

By Jamie Shreeve

4.4 Million Years Ago

Owen Lovejoy's first glimpse of the female who would preoccupy him for the next 14 years left him cold. It was 1995, and Lovejoy, a comparative anatomist at Kent State University in Ohio, was getting a privileged peek at the freshly excavated skeleton of Ardipithecus ramidus in the National Museum of Ethiopia in Addis Ababa. Some of the bones were badly squashed.

"My first thought was, why did they bring us over here to look at roadkill?" Lovejoy recalls. "It took about ten minutes to realize that all the important parts were there. My second thought was, Jesus Christ, who could have predicted this?"

Over the years, as Ardi's bones were freed from their rock-hard matrix and reconstructed, Lovejoy's astonishment would only grow. It had long been assumed that the future one probed into the human evolutionary past, the more our ancestors would look like our closest living relatives the chimpanzees. At 4.4 million years, Ardi was over a million years older than the famous Lucky skeleton, which Lovejoy had also analyzed. Ar. ramidus didn't look like Lucy—but she didn't look like a chimpanzee either. Instead, she possessed a weird combination of very primitive traits seen before only in monkeys and extinct apes from the Miocene epoch and traits seen only in our own hominid lineage.

Consider Ardi's foot. All later hominids, including Lucy, have a big toe that lines up with the other toes, helping to provide the propulsive force in upright walking, long the hallmark of our lineage. Ardi's big toe instead splayed out to the side, like those of apes—the better to grasp on to limbs when clambering about in the trees. Yet Ardi's foot also contains a small bone called the osperoneum—retained in the hominid lineage from ancient apes and monkeys but almost never seen in chimps and gorillas—that keeps the bottom of the foot more rigid. Lovejoy and his colleagues believe that this rigidity enabled Ar. ramidus to walk upright on the ground, using its four aligned toes to provide the levering "toe off" that propels a bipedal stride.

Ardi's pelvis also bears witness to a primitive primate caught in the act of becoming human. The human pelvis has undergone a major overhaul to adapt it for upright walking—a locomotor juggling act requiring one limb or the other to be suspended in the air while the other pushes forward. As far back as Lucy 3.2 million years ago, our hip bones had become broader and shorter to enlarge attachment areas for gluteal muscles that stabilize the supporting hip joint. In contrast, chimp pelvises are narrow and long and provide more rigid support for climbing but force chimps to lurch side to side when walking upright. Ardi's upper pelvis is short and broad and shows other features rarely seen except also in gorillas, which separated from out lineage even farther in the past, it has long been thought that it represents the primitive condition that out own ancestors passed through on their way to walking upright. Ardi's hand utterly confounds that assumption. Though her fingers are long, her palm is short and very flexible. This would have allowed her to walk on her palms on top of tree limbs, more like a monkey than any living ape, as well as hold on to branches well behind her head as she moved along limbs.

Combined with the other very primitive traits in *Ar. ramidus*, this monkey-like hand holds enormous repercussions for understanding our origins. If Ardi's discoverers are right, our ancestors never passed through a chimp-like, knuckle-walking phase on their way to walking upright. To argue that they did so would require that very early in our lineage we developed a chimp-like tool kit of adaptations—and then lost them all again and reverted to the primitive condition by the time *Ar. ramidus* was walking around. This is highly unlikely.

Still, given all the extremely primitive traits, some researchers argue that Ar. Ramidus isn't really a hominid in the first place. Terry Harrison of New York University, for instance, points out that there was a tremendous diversity of ape species throughout most of Africa and Eurasia in the Miocene epoch, between 23 and 5 million years ago.

"Perhaps it was just one of those apes running around, rather than the one that gave rise to hominins," says Harrison in response. Lovejoy points to more than two dozen distinct traits that link *Ar. ramidus* exclusively to later hominids-which, if

gotten around very well on two feet, especially with that widely divergent big toe.

"That ain't the foot of a biped!" comments William Jungers, an evolutionary morphologist at Stony Brook University. "Ardi has one of the most divergent big toes you can imagine. How did she get up in the trees without vertically climbing the trunks? Did she fly up there?" Why, asks Jungers, would an animal fully adapted to quadrupedal movement in trees elect to walk bipedally on the ground?

Lovejoy has a provocative answer to Jungers's question: sex. Lovejoy views the origins of bipedalism as the consequence of an epochal shift in social behavior. A key part of his theory is not something gained in our lineage but something lost: those daggerlike male canine teeth of apes, so effective as weapons against other males vying for mating opportunities. Males of virtually all living and extinct apes have large, pointed canines that sharpen by honing against their lower teeth. Hominid male canines are much smaller, more like a female's. Canines from 2 t individuals were found in the *Ar. ramidus* sediments of the Middle Awash, presumably both male and female. All share the hominid pattern.

Instead of gaining access to females through conflict with other males, in Lovejoy's view, a male *Ar. ramidus* would supply a targeted female and her offspring with high-fat, high-protein foods, gaining her sexual favors exclusively in return-a reproductive strategy that ensured the children he was providing for were his own. This would require, however, that the male's hands be freed from their role in quadrupedal locomotion so they could carry back the food. Bipedality may have been a poor way for *Ar. ramidus* to get around, but through its contribution to the "sex for food" contract, it would have been an excellent way to bear more offspring. And in evolution, of course, more offspring is the name of the game.

Whatever the reason for Ardi's incipient bipedality—if that's what it was—a mere 200,000 years later Lucy's genus, *Australopithecus,* appeared in the same region—fully bipedal, like all the hominids that would follow. Did primitive, splay-toed *Ar. ramidus* undergo some accelerated change in those 200,000 years and emerge as the ancestor of all later hominids? Or was it a relict species that carried its quaint mosaic of primitive and advanced traits with it into extinction?

"These finds are incredibly important, and given the state of preservation of the bones, what the discoverers did was nothing short of heroic," says Jungers. "But this is just the beginning of the story."

Brothers in Arms

By Jane Bosveld

Did We Mate with the Neanderthals, or Did We Murder Them?

Aiming his crossbow, Steven Churchill leaves no more than a two-inch gap between the freshly killed pig and the tip of his spear. His weapon of choice is a bamboo rod attached to a sharpened stone, modeled after the killing tools wielded by early modern humans some 50,000 years ago, when they cohabited in Eurasia with their large-boned relatives, the Neanderthals. Churchill, an evolutionary anthropologist at Duke University, is doing an experiment to see if a spear thrown by an early modern human might have killed Shanidar 3, a roughly 40-year-oid Neanderthal male whose remains were uncovered in the 1950s in Shanidar Cave in northeastern Iraq. Anthropologists have long debated about a penetrating wound seen in Shanidar 3's rib cage: Was he injured by another Neanderthal in a fight—or was it an early modern human who went after him?

"Anyone who works on the ribs of Shanidar 3 wonders about this," Churchill says.

The possibility that early humans attacked, killed, and drove small bands of Neanderthals to extinction has intrigued anthropologists and fascinated the public ever since Neanderthal bones were first studied in the mid-19th century. At first naturalists were not sure what to make of the funny-looking humanlike bones. But with publication of Darwin's *On the Origin of Species*, the idea that the bones were from a species closely related to us began to make sense. Eventually scientists recognized that Neanderthals were an extinct species that shared a common ancestor (probably Homo heidelbergensis) with Homo sapiens. For thousands of years, Neanderthals were the only hominids living in Europe and parts of Asia. Then, around 50,000 years ago, early modern humans migrated into Europe from Africa. By 28,000 to 30,000 years ago, the Neanderthals had disappeared.

For more than a century after their discovery, our robust relatives were depicted as dumb brutes, but the Neanderthals have had something of a facelift in recent years. They are now considered to have been intelligent (as smart as early modern humans, some anthropologists think), perhaps red-haired and pale-skinned, and capable of speech. They might even have created their own language. The more we learn about Neanderthals, the more familiar they seem. But one deep mystery remains: Whatever happened to them, and why did they disappear?

There are many theories but not a lot of proof. That is why Churchill's study of Shanidar 3 and another study published this year about humans cannibalizing Neanderthals are essential. They add a few details to the shadowy picture we have of our long-lost cousins. Anthropologists have many interpretations. Maybe our direct ancestors and Neanderthals largely coexisted (as did many other overlapping hominid species before them), with occasional bouts of quasi-tribal warfare that ebbed strategy actually came from Churchill's colleague John Shea, a paleo-anthropologist at Stony Brook University in New York who reconstructs the behavior of prehistoric peoples by analyzing their stone tools. To understand how stone points are worn down when piercing flesh and bone, Shea had run a set of experiments, stabbing goat carcasses and then noting the damage to the tools.

Churchill hoped to compare the cuts on Shea's goat bones to the mark on Shanidar 3's rib. Unfortunately, the goat bones were so damaged by the blows that "it was impossible to analyze them," he says.

He concluded that he would nave to do his own experiments to replicate the physics of Shanidar 3's prehistoric wound. Neanderthals were the power-thrusters of the Paleolithic world, driving their heavy spears with great kinetic energy and momentum into bison, boar, and deer, if Shanidar 3 had been injured by such a thrust, If would suggest that he had gotten into a fight with another Neanderthal, or perhaps that he had been hurt in a hunting accident. But if the wound had resulted from a lighter spear—from a projectile deftly thrown at a distance, with less momentum and enemy—the attacker was most likely human. There is no evidence whatsoever that Neanderthals ever used throwing spears, Churchill says.

After inflicting a set of sample wounds on pig bones, which are close in terms of size and shape to those of Neanderthals and which were easily obtained from a nearby slaughterhouse), Churchill and his team of students spent an evening cleaning the bones by boiling them in hot water and Biz, a laundry detergent containing enzymes that

Eating the Neanderthal of Les Rois

The spearing of Shanidar 3 documents only the act of one individual against another. Paleontologist Fernando Ramirez Rozzi discovered something far more nefarious while comparing the jawbones of a Neanderthal child and an early modern human last year at the institute of Human Paleontology in Paris. Both mandibles, dating from about 30,000 years ago, had been excavated from a cave called Les Rois in southwestern France. Finding Neanderthal bones mixed in with human bones is in itself significant because it shows that early humans and Neanderthals truly did meet face-to-face.

Ramirez Rozzi thinks that some of the encounters may have been peaceful, but this one apparently was not. The Neanderthal jawbone exhibits cut marks made by a stone tool that mirrors those seen on a number of reindeer jawbones found nearby. The marks are distinctive indicators of slaughtering. Including repeated indentations in the bone where the tongues were cut out. It is clear that early humans were eating Neanderthals," Ramirez Rozzi says. The cut marks are also similar to ones noted a decade earlier on deer and Neanderthal bones found at Moula-Guercy, a Paleolithic site in southeastern France near the Rhone River. The cannibals in that instance, though, were other Neanderthals, not early humans.

Anthropologists suspect that there was never a huge population of Neanderthals', although we do not have enough evidence yet to know how many lived at any given time. That is why some scientists doubt there were frequent run-ins between

Neanderthals and humans. But Ramirez Rozzi disagrees. He thinks that Neanderthals and early humans met "on many occasions" and that some of those meetings were violent. "We can also say that, as with violent encounters between different peoples, on one of those violent meetings the loser—the Neanderthal—was eaten by the winner," he says.

The Last Days of the Neanderthals

The proven proximity has fostered a debate over whether humans and Neanderthals might have mated with each other as well. Ramirez Rozzi classifies Neanderthals as a separate species, Homo neanderthalensis, and therefore suspects that close relationships with early humans were rare. "I think early modern humans viewed Neanderthals as a different group, as the other," he says.

But Erik Trinkaus, a physical anthropologist at Washington University in St. Louis, thinks the two hominids had a much stronger connection. In fact, he controversially argues that Neanderthals did not really go extinct. Rather, he claims, they were absorbed into the larger, rapidly growing population of early humans migrating into Eurasia from Africa. "We will never know to what extent they were absorbed. The bottom line is that they were humans, and sex happens," he says.

Many of Trinkaus's colleagues dispute that idea. Svante Pääbo, who leads the Neanderthal Genome Project at the Max Planck institute in Germany, painstakingly sequenced samples of Neanderthal DNA and found little evidence of their genes in us. His result implies that there was minimal interbreeding. "But so far we have only been able to see if humans have any genes from Neanderthals," he says. "We are now starting to look to see if there are genes in Neanderthals that came from modern humans."

Most anthropologists interpret the disappearance of the Neanderthals some 30,000 years ago as a true extinction. They are just not sure why it occurred, "My gut feeling," says Neanderthal expert Francesco d'Errico, director of the National Center for Scientific Research in France, "is that the Neanderthal extinction went on for several millennia and was modulated, but not determined, by climatic changes."

Indeed, the era between 65,000 and 25,000 years ago, toward the end of the Paleolithic, was a time of major volcanic eruptions, along with extremes of climate that included rapid shifts in temperature accompanied by alternately creeping and contracting glaciers across many regions of Eurasia. "This put a lot of stress on plant and animal life," says archaeologist Steve Kuhn of the University of Arizona. "Habitats were shrinking. Some researchers believe that everything was changing faster than the Neanderthals' capacity to adjust to them."

There also probably were not very many Neanderthals, and their small population may have played a role in their extinction. "Rare animals can be wiped out by climatic stress and competition more easily than animals that are common," Kuhn says. Kuhn and his colleague and spouse, archaeologist Mary Stiner, also suggest that the Neanderthals' social structure put them at risk. Unlike early human hunter-gatherer groups, Neanderthals concentrated almost entirely on hunting big game, as evidenced by the abundance of large animal bones in Neanderthal archaeological sites. At these sites there is also an absence of technology for grinding or crushing plant foods to extract their nutrients, which is essential to the lifestyle of foragers. "They engaged their entire group—men, women and children—in hunting big game," Kuhn says. Involving the whole tribe in hunting worked well until the climate changed and competition showed up in the form of early humans. Homo sapiens's division of labor allowed women and children to focus on small game and gathering while men went after the larger prey. In tough times, Kuhn argues, this diversified diet gave early humans a survival edge.

It is impossible to know exactly how major a role human aggression played in the Neanderthals' disappearance. The groups undoubtedly competed for resources, though, and evidently humans sometimes attacked or even ate Neanderthals. The death of Shanidar 3 may thus have foreshadowed the fate of his entire species.

Shanidar 3's death remains a mystery.

Close Encounters of the Neanderthal Kind

"If you met a Neanderthal in a crowd of people, you might think they were a little funny-looking, but that's it. On the other hand, if you went into a town and everyone there was a Neanderthal, you would start to notice that they all looked different

"The bad reputation of Neanderthals is a by-product of Victorian views of evolution and extant humans—in fact, 19th-century white, affluent Englishmen—as sitting at the top of the 'ladder of life.'" —João Zilhão, archaeologist, University of Bristol

"Does our fascination with Shanidar 3 have something to do with our recent history of colonization and violence toward one another?" —Steven Churchill, anthropologist, Duke University

This Is the Face That's Changing a Thousand Minds

By Rick Gore

This is that's changing a thousand minds. It could be the face of the

And it's not what anyone expected. This 1.75-million-year-old pioneer, found last year beneath the ruins of a medieval town called Dmanisi in the republic of Georgia, had a tiny brain—not nearly the size scientists thought our ancestors needed to migrate into a new land. And its huge canine teeth and thin brow look too apelike for an advanced hominid, the group that includes modern humans and their ancestors. Along with other fossils and tools found at the site, this skull reopens so many questions about our ancestry that one scientist muttered: "They ought to put it back in the ground."

"It looks like the first people out of Africa came out with a little pea brain." Philip Rightmire of Bingham ton University, who has spent a career measuring the bumps on the skulls and spaces between the eyes of a hodgepodge of fossils known as *Homo erectus,* is pronouncing a paradigm shift. Like most paleoanthropologists, Rightmire has long regarded *Homo erectus* as the first pioneer—the first hominid to leave Africa. But the new skull found under a medieval village in the republic of Georgia is shaking that assumption, if not the trunk of our family tree. Maybe the first human to walk out of Africa wasn't a classic *Homo erectus,* a creature with a big brain and the ability to make complex stone tools. Maybe something more primitive—a kind of missing link between *Homo erectus* and the first member of our genus, *Homo habilis*—got out earlier. Rightmire's world has been turned upside down—and he seems almost gleeful.

So is David Lordkipanidze, the Georgian scientist and National Geographic Society grantee whose team found the skull, as he pulls out casts of the skull and a matching jawbone at the Society's headquarters in Washington, D.C. Skulls of humans this old are rare. And they don't usually look this good. "This is perhaps the most complete skull of a hominid of this age," says Lordkipanidze. Most of the fragile bones of its face are intact. The skull and the jawbone have many of their teeth, including a wicked set of canines that makes them look like props from *I Was a Teenage Werewolf.* The interior

The new Dmanisi skull has a mosaic of features from other species.

million years ago, the earliest undisputed evidence of humans outside African. Those dates at first surprised a skeptical scientific community. In the early 1990s most scientists thought *Homo erectus* hadn't departed Africa until around a million years ago.

Then last season, while visiting another dig in western Georgia, Dato got a call on his cell phone from Dmanisi: Another skull was coming out of the earth. Dato rushed back. The skull he saw half-buried in the dirt astonished him.

Usually fossil skills are crashed almost beyond recognition, but this one looked almost as complete as a skull you find at a 21st century crime scene. And it didn't look like *Homo erectus*. Its browridge seemed too thin. It didn't have much of a nose, and it had those werewolf canines, holdavers from our apelike ancestors. And its brain case was tiny less than two thirds the size of an average *Homo erectus*. If brain size is a measure of intelligence, as scientists have long believed then this hominid from Georgia probably wasn't nearly as smart as a typical *Homo erectus*.

To Dato the new skill had the chimplike face of *Homo habilis* a small hominid with long, dangling arms who made primitive stone tools 2.1 million years ago. The implications left Dato reeling. "These hominids arc more primitive than we thought," he said. "We have a new puzzle." Could it be that the first human intercontinental traveler wasn't a classic *Homo erectus*?

Homo erectus in Africa was a tall creature with long strides and a big brain, built much like us. *Homo habilis*, on the other hand, had short legs and long arms. *Homo habilis* tool sites found in Africa suggest that the species lived only near reliable simple choppers and scrapers like those that *Homo habilis* used in Africa to cut small pieces off carcasses or pound marrow from bone. Maybe scavenging provided all the nutrients a migrant needed.

And the tiny brain of the Dmanisi skull? Scientists maybe forced to reexamine the connection between brain size and intelligence. "There's no reason to downgrade these early-Georgians on the IQ scale," says Philip Right-mire. "They took a long hike, and they made it." Maybe, says Rightmire, brain size by itself doesn't matter, and it's instead the ratio of gray matter to the rest of the body that determines intelligence. In other words, these small-brained humans might have done more with less.

Dato hopes soon to find bones from the rest of the skull's body; only then will we know whether this animal was built like *Homo erectus*, *Homo habilis*, or something in between (for now Dato still cautiously calls the Dmanisi hominids *Homo erectus*). But one thing is certain: The new find at Dmanisi complicates most models for *Homo erectus* using its brave new brain to march into Eurasia. *Homo erectus* in Java and China was heavier and more robust than it was in Africa. Moreover, Asian *erectus* did not have hand axes. So, it's possible that *Homo erectus* evolved from this primitive Dmanisi stock somewhere in Asia and then moved back to Africa. Maybe there were multiple migrations back and forth.

Maybe, suggests Milford Wolpoff of the University of Michigan, we should scrap the idea of *Homo erectus* entirely and simply say that everything after homo *habilis* is *Homo sapiens*. The remarkable variability of the specimens found at Dmanisi may support this radical revision of Homo's genealogy.

The Dmanisi team has found parts of as many as six individuals in the same layers of rock. Among them is an enormous jawbones it belonged to an individual who must have been significantly bigger than the others. It's possible that there were several species of hominids here, but Dato thinks that's unlikely—the fossils were found close to each other and different hominid species don't tend to be found together. If they're the same species, then the size differences need to be explained some other way. Perhaps the big mandible belonged to an old male, and like gorillas today Dmanisi males were much larger than females. Or perhaps our ancestors were as variable in size as humans are today. Why not? After all, Shaquille O'Neal and Danny DeVito are members of the same species. Is it possible that the scientists who have given new species names to every early *Homo* find with significant differences have made our family tree more complicated than it really is?

These questions please Dato, and being a Georgia patriot, he's also pleased that such critical insights into humanity's first footstep into a new world began to emerge at the same time his nation was struggling to establish its independence in the early 1990s. "It was it very hard time in our history," he says. "Dmanisi was our first major international science project. Now *this* has happened. It's luck, you see, really big luck."

The Downside of Upright

By Jennifer Ackerman

The agility and brainpower we've gained since our ancestors stood up on two feet haven't come without evolutionary trade-offs; a plethora of aches and pains that make it hard to be human.

We humans are odd creatures: tailless bipeds with sinuous spines, song limbs, arched feet, agile hands, and enormous brains. Our bodies are a mosaic of features shaped by natural selection over vast period of time-both exquisitely capable and deeply flawed. We can stand, walk, and run with grace and endurance, but we suffer aching feet and knee injuries; we can twist and torque our spines, and yet most of us are plagued by back trouble at some point in our fives: we can give birth to babies with big brains, but only through great pain and risk. Scientists have long sought to answer the question of how our bodies came to be the way they are. Now, using new methods from a variety of disciplines, they are discovering that many of the flaws in our "design" have a common theme. They arise primarily from evolutionary compromises that came about when our ancestors stood upright-the first step in the long path to becoming human.

A Tight Squeeze

In Karen Rosenberg's laboratory at the University of Delaware, a room packed with the casts of skulls and bones of chimpanzees, gibbons, and other primates, one model stands out: It's a life-size replica of a human female pelvic skeleton mounted on a platform. There is also a fetal skull with a flexible gooseneck wire. The idea is to simulate the human birth process by manually moving the fetal head through the pelvis.

It looks easy enough.

"Go ahead, try it" Rosenberg says.

Turn the little oval skull face-forward, and it drops neatly into the pelvic brim, the beginning of the birth canal. But then it jams against the protrusions of the ischial bones (those that bear the burden during a long car ride). More shoving and rotating, and it's quickly apparent that the skull must traverse a passage that seems smaller than itself, cramped not only by the ischial bones but also by the coccyx, the bottom of the tailbone, which pokes into the lower pelvic cavity. Only by maneuvering the skull to face sideways in the middle of the canal and then giving it a firm push, does it move a centimeter or two-before it gets hung up again. Twist it, jostle it: The thing won't budge, Rosenberg guides my hand to turn the skull around to face backward, and then, with a hard shove, the stubborn cranium finally exits the birth canal.

"Navigating the birth canal is probably the most gymnastic maneuver most of us will ever make in life," says Rosenberg, chair of the university's department of anthropology. It's a trick all right, especially if there's no guiding hand to twirl and ram the skull.

Jennifer Ackerman, "The Downside of Upright," from *National Geographic*, vol. 210, no. 1; July 2006, pp. 126–145. Copyright © 2006 by National Geographic Society. Permission to reprint granted by the publisher.

nurses to safely deliver my firstborn.

Birth is an ordeal for women everywhere, according to a review of birthing patterns in nearly 300 cultures around the world by Rosenberg and colleague Wenda Trevathan, an anthropologist at New Mexico State University. "Not only is labor difficult," Rosenberg says, "but because of the design of the female pelvis, infants exit the birth canal with the back of their heads against the pubic bones, facing in the opposite direction from the mother. This makes it tough for her to reach down and guide the baby as it emerges without damaging its spine-and also inhibits her ability to clear the baby's breathing passage or to remove the umbilical cord from around its neck. That's why women everywhere seek assistance during labor and delivery."

Compared with humans, most primates have an easier time, Rosenberg says. A baby chimpanzee, for instance, is born quickly: entering, passing through, and leaving its mother's pelvis in a straight shot and emerging face-up so that its mother can pull it forward and lift it toward her breast, in chimps and other primates, the oval birth canal is oriented the same way from beginning to end. In humans, it's a flattened oval one way and then it shifts orientation 90 degrees so that it's flattened the other way. To get through, the infant's head and shoulders have to align with that shifting oval it's this changing cross-sectional shape of the passageway that makes human birth difficult and risky, Rosenberg says, not just for babies but also for mothers. A hundred years ago, childbirth was a leading cause of death for women of childbearing age.

Why do we possess a birth canal of such Byzantine design? "The human female pelvis is not the type of system you would invent if you were designing it. But evolution is clearly a tinkerer, not an engineer; it has to work with yesterday's model.

Yesterday's Model

Humans come from a long line of ancestors, from reptile to mammal to ape, whose skeletons were built to carry their weight on all fours. Our ape ancestors probably evolved around 20 million years ago from small primates that carried themselves horizontally. Over the next several million years, some apes grew larger and began to use their arms to hold overhead branches and, perhaps, to reach for fruit. Then, six or seven million years ago, our ancestors stood up and began to move about on their hind legs. By the time the famous Lucy (Australopithecus afarensis) appeared in East Africa 3.2 million years ago, they had adopted walking as their chief mode of getting around.

It was a radical shift. "Bipedalism is a unique and bizarre form of locomotion," says Craig Stanford, an anthropologist at the University of Southern California. "Of more than 250 species of primates, only one goes around on two legs." Stanford and many other scientists consider bipedalism the key defining feature of being human. "Some may think it's our big brain," Stanford says, "but the rapid expansion of the human brain didn't begin until less than two million years ago, millions of years after we got upright and began using tools. Bipedalism was the initial adaptation that paved the way for others."

Evolutionary biologists agree that shifts in behavior often drive changes in anatomy. Standing upright launched a cascade of anatomical alterations. The biomechanics of upright walking is so drastically different from quadrupedal locomotion that bones from the neck down had to change. The skull and spine were realigned, bringing the head and torso into a vertical line over the hips and feet. To support the body's weight and absorb the forces of upright locomotion, joints in limbs and the spine enlarged and the foot evolved an arch. As for the pelvis, if morphed from the ape's long, thin paddle into a wide, flat saddle shape, which thrust the weight of the trunk down through the legs and accommodated the attachment of large muscles. This improved the stability of the body and the efficiency of walking upright but severely constricted the birth canal.

All of these architectural changes, seen clearly In the fossil record, did not happen overnight. They came gradually, over many generations and over long periods of time, in small steps favored by natural selection.

Upright Citizens

Consider the simple human act of walking or running. At his laboratory in the anthropology department at Harvard University, Dan Lieberman does just that, using biomechanical studies to see how we use our body parts in various aspects of movement. As a volunteer subject in one of his experiments last fall, I was wired up and put through paces on a treadmill. On my feet were pressure sensors to show my heel and toe strikes. Electromyographic sensors revealed the firing of my muscles, and accelerometers and rate gyros on my head detected its pitching, rolling, and yawing movements. Small silver foam balls attached to my joints-ankle, knee, hip, elbow, shoulder acted as reflectors for three infrared cameras mapping in three-dimensional space the location of my limb segments.

These biomechanical windows on walking and running illuminate just how astonishing a feat of balance, coordination, and efficiency is upright locomotion. The legs on a walking human body act not unlike inverted pendulums. Using a stiff leg as

a point of support, the body swings up and over it in an arc, so that the potential energy gained in the rise roughly equals the kinetic energy generated in the descent. By this trick the body stores and recovers so much of the energy used with each stride that it reduces its own workload by as much as 65 percent.

The key lies in our human features: the ability to fully extend our knees; the way our lower back curves forward and our thighbone slopes inward from hip to knee so that our feet straddle our center of gravity; and the action of the gluteal abductors, the muscles attached to the pelvis that contract to prevent us from toppling over sideways mid-stride when our weight is on a single foot.

In running, we shift from this swinging pendulum mode to a bouncy pogo-stick mode, using the tendons in our legs as elastic springs. Lieberman's recent studies with Dennis Bramble of the University of Utah suggest that running—which our ancestors mastered some two million years ago—was instrumental in the evolution of several features, including our extra leg tendons, our relatively hairless skin and copious sweat glands (which facilitate cooling), and our enlarged gluteus maximus, the biggest muscle in the body, which wraps the rear end and acts to stabilize the trunk, preventing us from pitching forward. Now Lieberman is studying the role in upright locomotion of a tiny slip of muscle in the neck called the cleidocranial trapezius—all that remains of a massive shoulder muscle in chimps and other apes—which steadies our head during running, preventing if from bobbling.

Watching the graphs from the experiment on a computer screen, one can't help but marvel at the effectiveness of the system, the little cleidocranial portion of the trapezius steadying the head; the regular pumping action of arms and shoulders stabilizing the body; the consistent springlike rhythms of our long-legged stride.

"Compare this with the chimp," Lieberman says, "Chimps pay a hefty price in energy for being built the way they are. They can't extend their knees and lock their legs straight, as humans can. Instead, they have to use muscle power to support their body

Two-legged walking in a chimp is an occasional, transitory behavior. In humans, it is a way of life, one that carries with it myriad benefits, perhaps chief among them, freed hands. But upright posture and locomotion come with a host of uniquely human maladies.

Achilles' Back

An old friend of mine, a former politician from West Virginia, has difficulty remembering names. He saves himself from embarrassment with a simple trick: He delivers a hearty handshake and asks, "So how's your back?" Four times out of five he strikes gold. Names become unnecessary when the acquaintance, flattered by the personal inquiry, launches into a saga of lumbar pain, slipped disk, or mild scoliosis.

Back pain is one of the most common health complaints, accounting for more than 15 million doctor visits each year. That most of us will experience debilitating back pain at some point in our lives raises the question of the spine's design,

"The problem is that the vertebral column was originally designed to act as an arch," explains Carol Ward, an anthropologist and anatomist at the University of Missouri in Columbia. "When we became upright, it had to function as a weight-bearing column." To support our head and balance our weight directly over our hip joints and lower limbs, the spine evolved a series of S curves—a deep forward curve, or lordosis, in the lower back, and a backward curve, or kyphosis, in the upper back.

and effective for maintaining our balance and for bipedal locomotion," Ward says. "But the lower region of the column suffers from the excessive pressure and oblique force exerted on its curved structure by our upright posture."

Lean back, arching your spine. You're the only mammal in the world capable of this sort of backbend. Feel a cringing tightness in your lower back? That's the vertical joints between your vertebrae pressing against one another as their compressive load increases. The curvature in your lower spine requires that its building blocks take the shape of a wedge, with the thick part in the front and the thin part in the back. The wedge-shaped vertebrae are linked by vertical joints that prevent them from slipping out from one another.

"These joints are delicate structures and very complex," Ward says. "They allow our spines to move with great flexibility, to twist and bend and flex, pivoting on the disks between the vertebrae."

But in the lower back region, where the load is heaviest and the wedging most dramatic, strains such as heavy lifting or hyperextension (say, from doing the butterfly stroke or cleaning the gutters) can cause your lowest vertebrae to slip or squish together. When the vertebrae are pressured in this way, the disks between them may herniate, or bulge out, impinging on spinal nerves and causing pain. Or the pressure may pinch the dedicate structures at the back of the vertebrae, causing a fracture called spondylolysis, a problem for about one in twenty Americans.

No other primate experiences such back problems-except, Ward and Latimer say, our immediate ancestors. The two scientists have found fossil evidence that back trouble likely plagued our bipedal forebears. The bones of the Nariokotome boy, a young Homo erectus (a species preceding our own Homo sapiens) who lived some 1.5 million years ago, reveal that the youth suffered from scoliosis, a potentially devastating lateral curvature of the spine.

The cause of most scoliosis cases remains a mystery, Latimer says, but like spondylolysis, it appears linked to the spinal features associated with upright posture, particularly lordosis, the deep forward curvature and flexibility of our lower spine. "Because scoliosis occurs only in humans and our immediate bipedal ancestors, it appears likely that upright walking is at least partially to blame," he says.

Considering the pressures of natural selection, why are such seriously debilitating diseases still prevalent? Latimer suspects the answer lies in the importance of lordosis for upright walking: "Selection for bipedality must have been so strong in our early ancestors that a permanent lordosis developed despite the risk it carries for spondylolysis and other back disorders."

Disjointed

Liz Scarpelli's postural orientation is at the moment horizontal. Her leg is elevated in a surgical sling as Scott Dye, an orthopedic surgeon at California Pacific Medical Center, examines her knee with an arthroscope. The ghostly image of the joint-femur, tibia, and patella-appear magnified on a fiat screen above the gurney. An athletic woman of 51, a former gymnast and skier, Scarpelli is a physical therapist who works with patients to rehabilitate their joints after surgery. While demonstrating to one patient a technique for leg-strengthening knee squats, Scarpeili blew out her own knee for the third time. Dye's arthroscopic camera shows healthy bone and ligaments, but large chunks of cartilage float about like icebergs in the fluid spaces around the joint. Dye expertly scrapes up the pieces and sucks them out before sewing up the holes and moving on to the next five surgeries scheduled for the day.

To hear Scott Dye speak of it, the knee joint is among the greatest of nature's inventions, "a 360-million-year-old structure beautifully designed to do its job of transferring load between limbs." But it is also among the most easily injured joints in the human body; medical procedures involving knees total a million a year in the United States.

"In standing upright, we have imposed unprecedented forces on the knee, ankle, and foot," Bruce Latimer says. When we walk quickly or run, the forces absorbed by our lower limbs may approach several multiples of our own body weight. Moreover, our pelvic anatomy exerts so-called lateral pressure on our lower joints. Because of the breadth of our pelvis, our thighbone is angled inward toward the knee, rather than straight up and down, as it is in the chimp and other apes. This carrying angle ensures that the knee is brought well under the body to make us more stable.

"But nothing is free in evolution," Latimer says. "This peculiar angle means that there are forces on the knee threatening to destabilize it. In women, the angle is greater because of their wider pelvis, which explains why they are slower runners—the increased angle means that they're wasting maybe ten percent of their energy—and also why they tend to suffer more knee injuries."

Unlikely Feat

And where does the buck finally stop? What finally bears the full weight of our upright body? Two ridiculously tiny platforms.

"The human foot has rightfully been called the most characteristic peculiarity in the human body," says Will Harcourt-Smith, a paleontologist at the American Museum of Natural History. "For one thing, if has no thumblike opposable toe. We're the only primate to give up the foot as a grasping organ."

This was a huge sacrifice. The chimp's foot is a brilliantly useful and versatile feature, essential to tree climbing and capable of as much motion and manipulation as its hand. The human foot, by contrast, is a hyper-specialized organ, designed to do just two things, propel the body forward and absorb improving on another, all evolving toward perfection in Homo sapiens. But evolution doesn't evolve toward anything; it's a messy affair, full of diversity and dead ends. There were probably lots of ways of getting around on two feet."

Still, in all the fossil feet Harcourt-Smith studies, some type of basic human pattern is clearly present: a big toe aligned with the long axis of the foot, or a well-developed longitudinal arch, or in some cases a humanlike ankle joint—all ingenious adaptations but fraught with potential problems. "Because the foot is so specialized in its design," Harcourt-Smith says, "it has a very narrow window for working correctly. If it's a bit too flat or too arched, or if it turns in or out too much, you get the host of complications that has spurred the industry of podiatry." In people with a reduced arch, fatigue fractures often develop. In those with a pronounced arch, the ligaments that support the arch sometimes become inflamed, causing plantar fasciitis and heel spurs. When the carrying angle of the leg forces the big toe out of alignment, bunions may form—more of a problem for women than men because of their wider hips.

And that's not all.

"One of the really remarkable aspects of the human foot, compared with the chimp and other apes, is the relatively large size of its bones, particularly the heel bone," Bruce Latimer notes. A 350-pound male gorilla has a smaller heel bone than does a 100-pound human female—however, the gorilla bone is a lot more dense." While the ape heel is solid with thick cortical bone, the human heel is puffed up and covered with only a paper-thin layer of cortical bone; the rest is thin latticelike cancellous bone. This enlargement of cancellous bone is pronounced in an accelerated rate of bone mineral loss—or osteopenia—as we age, which may eventually lead to osteoporosis and hip and vertebral fractures."

What Do We Stand For?

We humans gave up stability and speed. We gave up the foot as a grasping tool. We gained spongy bones and fragile joints and vulnerable spines and difficult, risky births that led to the deaths of countless babies and mothers. Given the trade-offs, the aches and pains and severe drawbacks associated with bipedalism, why get upright in the first place?

A couple of chimps named Jack and Louie may offer some insights. The chimps are part of an experiment by a team of scientists to explore the origin of bipedalism in our hominin ancestors.

Theories about why we got upright have run the gamut from freeing the arms of our ancestors to carry babies and food to reaching hitherto inaccessible fruits. "But," says Mike Sockol of the University of California, Davis, "one factor had to play a part in every scenario: the amount of energy required to move from point to point. If you can save energy while gathering your food supply, that energy can go into growth and reproduction."

Paleogeographical studies suggest that at the time our ancestors first stood upright, perhaps six to eight million years ago, their food supplies were becoming more widely dispersed. "Rainfall in equatorial East Africa was declining," Sockol says, "and the forest was changing from dense and closed to more open, with more distance between food resources. If our ape ancestors had to roam farther to find adequate food, and doing so on two legs saved energy, then those individuals who moved across the ground more economically gained an advantage."

To test the theory that the shift to two feet among our ancestors may have been spurred by energy savings, Sockol and his colleagues are looking at the energy cost of locomotion in the chimp. The chimp is a good model, Sockol says, not just because it's similar to us in body size and skeletal features and can walk both bipedaliy and quadrupedally, but also because the majority of evidence suggests that the last common ancestor of chimps and humans who first stood upright was chimplike. By understanding how a chimp moves, and whether it expends more or less energy in walking upright or on all fours (knuckle-walking), the scientists hope to gain insight Info our ancestors' radical change in posture.

Jack and Louie and several other young adult chimps have been trained by skillful professional handlers to walk and run on a treadmill, both on two legs and on four. One morning, lack sits patiently in his trainer's lap while Sockol's collaborators, Dave Raichien and Herman Pontzer of Harvard University, paint small white patches on his joints--the equivalent of those silver balls I wore on Dan lieberman's treadmill. Only occasionally does jack steal a surreptitious lick of the sweet white stuff. Once he's marked, he jumps on the treadmill and runs along on two legs for a few minutes, then drops to four. Every so often, his trainer hands him a fruit snack, which Jack balances on his lower lip, thrust out as far as it will go, before rolling the fruit forward and flicking it into his mouth. For a set time, Jack breathes into a small mask connected to equipment that gathers information on how much oxygen he consumes-a measure of energy expenditure-while the movements of his limbs (marked by those white dots) are monitored with cameras to help the scientists understand how the energy is being used.

Once the scientists have refined their model for how things work in the chimp—for what limb movements are used in the two types of locomotion and how each consumes energy—they hope to apply this model to the fossils of our ancestors. "We use the biomechanical data to determine the types of anatomical changes that would have reduced energy expenditure," Raichlen explains. "Then we look at the fossil record and ask, do we see these changes? If we do, that's a pretty good clue that we're looking at selection for reduced energy costs in our ancestors who became bipedal. That's the dream."

Scientists are the first to admit that much work needs to be done before we fully understand the origins of bipedalism. But whatever drove human ancestors to get upright in the first place—reaching for fruit or traveling farther in search of it, scanning the horizon for predators or transporting food to family—the habit stuck. They eventually evolved the ability to walk and run long distances. They learned to hunt and scavenge meat. They created and manipulated a diverse array of tools. These were all essential steps in evolving a big brain and a human intelligence, one that could make poetry and music and mathematics, assist in difficult childbirth, develop sophisticated technology, and consider the roots of its own quirky and imperfect upright being.

Chapter 5

Human Variation

Human Variation, like Human Evolution, is one of the cornerstones of biological anthropology. In most four-field programs of anthropology, students are required to have a basic knowledge of human biodiversity. Understanding the importance of biodiversity is as critical as knowing the importance of cultural diversity among humans. In the past, human biodiversity was referred to as race. In fact, in many communities, and among Americans in daily conversation, it is still referred to as race. In these exchanges, race may still carry notions of racism and bias associated with the term. Unfortunately, much of these incorrect concepts come from past biological studies that were done during the late 19th and early 20th centuries. Even though much of this work is no longer considered valid science, these ideas are ingrained in the public's thinking. It is difficult for folks to let them go.

Today, biological anthropologists teach the principles of biodiversity among humans as a means of explaining why our species (*Homo sapiens*) is as successful as it is. We have managed to adapt to a wide range of ecological zones (high altitude, cold and hot deserts, tropical rain forests, coastal areas, and grasslands, to name a few). Because of our flexibility as a species in coping successfully with so many eco-zones, we are a polymorphic and polytypic species—meaning we have a wide range of biological expressions by which we survive.

The articles in this section of the lab reader are here to illustrate how humans have managed to survive under some extreme conditions, via climate, environment, or by facing diseases or health problems related to dietary conditions. In doing so, humans overcome these issues with a combination of biological features (some seen as allelic expressions of genetic traits, and some as phenotypic characteristics) and cultural means. As a result, biological anthropologists approach the study of how humans adapt by employing what is known as a bio-cultural approach. These act as a theory through which we can understand how humans navigate through the stressors that challenge them, as they attempt to survive and reproduce the next generation.

How We Are Evolving

By Jonatahan Pritchard

New analyses suggest that recent human evolution has followed a different course than biologists would have expected.

Thousands of years ago humans moved for the first time into the Tibetan plateau, a vast expanse of steppelands that towers some 14,000 feet above sea level. Although these trailblazers would have had the benefit of entering a new ecosystem free of competition with other people, the low oxygen levels at that altitude would have placed severe stresses on the body, resulting in chronic altitude sickness and high infant mortality. Earlier this year a flurry of genetic studies identified a gene variant that is common in Tibetans but rare in other populations. This variant, which adjusts red blood cell production in Tibetans, helps to explain how Tibetans adapted to those harsh conditions. The discovery, which made headlines around the world, provided a dramatic example of how humans have undergone rapid biological adaptation to new environmental circumstances in the recent past. One study estimated that the beneficial variant spread to high frequency within the past 3,000 years—a mere instant in evolutionary terms.

The Tibet findings seemed to bolster the notion that our species has undergone considerable biological adaptation of this sort since it first left Africa perhaps 60,000 years ago (estimates range from 50,000 to 100,000 years ago). The transition to high altitude is just one of many environmental challenges Homo sapiens encountered as it migrated from the hot grasslands and shrublands of East Africa to frigid tundras, steamy rain forests and sunbaked deserts—practically every terrestrial ecosystem and climate zone on the planet. To be sure, much of human adaptation was technological—to combat the cold, for instance, we made clothing. But prehistoric technology alone could not have been enough to overcome thin mountain air, the ravages of infectious disease and other environmental obstacles. In these circumstances, adaptation would have to occur by genetic evolution rather than through technological solutions. It was reasonable to expect, then, that surveys of our genomes would reveal considerable evidence of novel genetic mutations that have spread recently throughout different populations by natural selection—that is, because those who carry the mutations have more healthy babies who survive to reproduce than those who do not.

Six years ago my colleagues and I set out to look for the imprints of these profound environmental challenges on the human genome. We wanted to figure out how humans have evolved since our predecessors set out on their relatively recent global journey. To what extent do populations in disparate parts of the world differ genetically because natural selection recently adapted them to different environmental pressures, as in the case of the Tibetans? What proportion of these genetic a beneficial mutation spread through a population long ago in response to a local environmental pressure and then was carried into faraway locales as the population expanded into new territories. For example, some gene variants involved in determining light skin color, an adaptation to reduced sunlight, are distributed according to ancient migration routes, rather than just latitude. That these ancient selection signals have persisted over millennia without new environmental pressures overwriting them indicates that natural selection often operates at a far more leisurely pace than scientists had envisioned. The rapid evolution of a major gene in the Tibetans, it appears, is not typical.

As an evolutionary biologist, I am often asked whether humans are still evolving today. We certainly are. But the answer to the question of how we are changing is far more complicated. Our data suggest that the classic natural selection scenario, in which a single beneficial humans in the past 60,000 years. Rather this mechanism of evolutionary change usually uncommon situation once our ancestors started globe-trotting and the pace of technological innovation began accelerating.

Already these findings are helping to refine our understanding not only of recent human evolution but also of what our collective future might hold. For a number of the challenges currently facing our species—global climate change and many infectious diseases, for example—natural selection probably occurs too slowly to help us much. Instead we are going to have to rely on culture and technology.

billion pairs of DNA nucleotides, or letters," that serve as an instruction manual for how to assemble a human [see box on next page]. The manual is now known to contain a parts list of about 20,000 genes-strings of DNA letters that spell out the information required to build proteins. (Proteins, which include enzymes, do much of the work in cells.) About 2 percent of the human genome encodes proteins, and a roughly similar amount seems to be involved in gene regulation. Most of the rest of the genome has no known role

Overall the genomes of any two people are extremely similar, differing in only about one out of every 1,000 nucleotide pairs. Sites where one nucleotide pair substitutes for another are referred to as single-nucleotide polymorphisms, or SNPs (pronounced "snips"), and the alternative versions of the DNA at each SNP are called alleles. Because most of the genome does not encode proteins or regulate genes, most SNPs probably have no measurable effect on the individual. But if a SNP occurs in a region of the genome that does have a coding or regulating function, it may affect the structure or function of a protein or where and how much of the protein is made. In this way, SNPs can conceivably modify almost any trait, be it height, eye color, ability to digest milk, or susceptibility to diseases such as diabetes, schizophrenia, malaria and HIV.

When natural selection strongly favors a particular allele, it becomes more common In the population with each generation, white the disfavored allele becomes less common. Eventually, if the environment remains stable, the beneficial allele will spread until everyone in the population carries it, at which point it has become fixed in that group.

This process typically takes many generations, if a person with two copies of the beneficial allele produces 10 percent more children and someone with one copy produces 5 percent more, on average, than someone without the beneficial allele, then it will take that allele about 200 generations, or roughly 5,000 years, to increase in frequency from 1 percent of the population to 99 percent of it. In theory, a helpful allele could become fixed in as little as a few hundred years if it conferred an extraordinarily large advantage. Conversely, a less advantageous allele could take many thousands of years to spread.

It would be great if in our efforts to understand recent human evolution, we could obtain DNA samples from ancient remains and actually track the changes of favored alleles over time. But DNA usually degrades quickly in ancient samples, thereby hindering this approach. Thus, my research group and a number of others around the world have developed methods of examining genetic variation in modern-day humans for signs of natural selection that has happened in the past.

One such tactic is to comb DNA data from many different people for stretches that show few differences in SNP alleles within a population. When a new beneficial mutation propagates rapidly through a group because of natural selection, it takes a surrounding chunk of the chromosome with it in a process called genetic hitchhiking. As the frequency of the beneficial allele increases in the group over time, so, too, do the frequencies of nearby "neutral" and nearly neutral alleles that do not affect protein structure or amount appreciably but ride along with the selected allele. The resulting reduction or elimination of SNP variation in the region of the genome containing a beneficial allele is termed a selective sweep. The spread of selected alleles by natural selection can also leave other distinctive patterns in the SNP data: if an existing allele suddenly proves particularly helpful when a population finds itself in new circumstances, that allele can reach high frequency (while remaining rare in other populations) without necessarily generating a hitchhiking signal.

Over the past few years multiple studies, including one my colleagues and I published in 2006, have identified several hundred genome signals of apparent natural selection that occurred within the past 60,000 years or so-that is, since H. sapiens left Africa. In a few of these cases, scientists have a pretty good grasp on the selective pressures and the adaptive benefit of the favored allele. For example, among dairy-farming populations in Europe, the Middle East and East Africa, the region of the genome that houses the gene for the lactase enzyme that digests lactose (the sugar in milk) shows clear signs of having been the target of strong selection, In most populations, babies are born with the ability to digest lactose, but the lactase gene turns off after weaning, leaving people unable to digest lactose as adults. Writing in the American Journal of Human Genetics in 2004, a team at the Massachusetts Institute of Technology estimated that variants of the lactase gene that remain active into adulthood achieved high frequency in European dairy-farming groups in just 5,000 to 10,000 years. In 2006 a group led by Sarah Tishkoff, who is now at the University of Pennsylvania, reported in *Nature Genetics* that they had found rapid evolution of the lactase gene in East African dairy-farming populations. These changes were surely an adaptive response to a new subsistence practice.

Researchers have also found pronounced signals of selection in at least half a dozen genes involved in determining skin, hair and eye color in non-Africans. Here, too, the selective pressure and adaptive benefit are clear. As humans moved out of their tropical homeland, they received reduced ultraviolet radiation from the sun. The body requires UV radiation to synthesize vitamin D, an essential nutrient, in the tropics, UV radiation is strong enough to penetrate dark skin in amounts needed for vitamin D synthesis. Not so in the higher latitudes. The need to absorb adequate amounts of vitamin D almost certainly drove the evolution of lighter skin color in these locales, and changes in these genes that bear signals of strong selection enabled that adaptive shift.

Selection signals also show up in a variety of genes that confer resistance to infectious diseases For instance, Pardis Sabeti of Harvard University and her colleagues have found a mutation in the so-called LARGE gene that has recently spread to high we do not yet know which circumstances favored the spread of the selected allele, nor do we know what effect the allele exerts on the people who harbor it. Until recently we and others interpreted these candidate signals to mean that there have been at least a few hundred very rapid selective sweeps within the past 15,000 years in several human populations that have been studied. But in newer work my colleagues and I have found evidence suggesting that instead most of these signals are not actually the result of very recent, rapid adaptation to local conditions at all.

Working with collaborators at Stanford University, we studied a massive SNP data set generated from DNA samples obtained from about 1.000 individuals from around the world. When we looked at the geographical distributions of selected alleles, we found that the most pronounced signals tend to fall into one of just three geographical patterns. First there are the so-called out-of-Africa sweeps, in which the favored allele and its hitchhikers exist at high frequency in all non-African populations [see box on preceding two pages]. This pattern suggests that the adaptive allele appeared and began to spread very shortly after humans left Africa but while they were still restricted to the Middle East— thus perhaps around 60,000 years ago—and was subsequently carried around the globe as humans migrated north and east. Then there are two other, more restricted, geographical patterns; the West Eurasian sweeps, in which a favored allele occurs at high frequency in ail of the populations of Europe, the Middle East, and Central and South Asia, but not elsewhere; and the East Asian sweeps, in which the favored allele is most common in East Asians,

to fine-tune those distributions to match modern environmental pressures. For example, one of the most important players in the adaptation to lighter skin color is a variant of the so-called SLC24A5 gene. Because it is an adaptation to reduced sunlight, one might expect its frequency in the population to increase with latitude and its distribution to be similar in people from North Asia and Northern Europe. Instead we see a West Eurasian sweep: the gene variant and the hitchhiking DNA that travels with if are common from Pakistan to France but essentially absent in East Asia-even in the northern latitudes. This distribution indicates that the beneficial variant arose in the ancestral population of the West Eurasians—after they diverged from the ancestors of the East Asians—who carried it throughout that region. Thus, natural selection drove the beneficial SLC24A5 allele to high frequency early on, but ancient population history helped to determine which populations today have it and which do not. (Other genes account for light skin in East Asians.)

A closer look at the selection signals in these and other data reveals another curious pattern. Most of the alleles with the most extreme frequency differences between populations—those that occur in nearly all Asians but no Africans, for example—do not exhibit the strong hitchhiking signals one would expect to see if natural selection swiftly drove these new alleles to high frequency. Instead these alleles seem to have propagated gradually during the roughly 60,000 years since our species set out from Africa.

In light of these observations, my collaborators and I now believe that textbook selective sweeps— in which natural selection drives an advantageous new mutation rapidly to fixation—have actually occurred fairly rarely in the time since the H. sapiens diaspora began. We suspect that natural selection usually acts relatively weakly on individual alleles, thus promoting them very slowly. As a result, most alleles experiencing selection pressure may attain high frequency only when the pressure persists for tens of thousands of years.

One Trait, Many Genes

Our conclusions may seem paradoxical: if it usually has taken 50,000, not 5,000, years for a helpful allele to spread through a population, how would humans ever manage to adapt quickly to new conditions? Although the best understood adaptations arise from changes in a single gene, it may be that most adaptations do not arise that way but rather stem from genetic variants having mild effects on hundreds or thousands of relevant genes from across the genome-which is to say they are polygenic. A series of papers published in 2008, for example, identified more than 50 different genes that influence human height, and certainly many more remain to be found. For each of these, one allele increases average height by just three to five millimeters compared with the other allele.

When natural selection targets human height-as has occurred in the pygmy populations that live in rain forest habitats in Africa, Southeast Asia and South America, where small body size may be an adaptation to the limited nutrition available in these environments-it may operate in large part by tweaking the allele frequencies of hundreds of different genes. If the "short" version of every height gene became just 10 percent more common, then most people in the population would quickly come to have more "short" alleles, and the population would be shorter overall. Even if the overall trait were under strong selection, the strength of selection on each individual height gene would still be weak. Because the selection acting on any one gene is weak, polygenic adaptations would not show up in genome studies as a classic signal of selection. Thus, it is possible that human genomes have undergone

more adaptive change recently than scientists can yet identify by examining the genome in the usual way.

Still Evolving?

As to whether humans are still evolving, it is difficult to catch natural selection in the act of shaping present-day populations. It is, however, easy to imagine traits that might be affected. Infectious diseases such as malaria and HIV continue to exert potent selection forces in the developing world. The handful of known gene variants that provide some measure of protection against these scourges are probably under strong selective pressure, because people who carry them are more likely to survive and live to have many more children than those who do not. A variant that shields carriers from the vivax form of malaria has become ubiquitous in many populations in sub-Saharan Africa. The variants that protect against HIV, meanwhile., could spread throughout sub-Saharan Africa in hundreds of years if the virus were to persist and continue to be thwarted by that resistance gene. But given that HIV is evolving faster than humans are, we are more likely to overcome that problem with technology (in the form of a vaccine) than with natural selection.

In the developed world relatively few people die between birth and adulthood, so strongest selection forces are probably those acting on genes that affect the number of children each person produces. In principle, any aspect of fertility or reproductive behavior that genetic variation affects could be the target of natural selection. Writing in the Proceedings of the National Academy of Sciences USA In 2009, Stephen C. Stearns of Yale University and his colleagues reported on the results of a study that identified six different traits in women that are associated with higher lifetime numbers of children and that all show intermediate to high heritably. Women with larger numbers of children, the team found, tend to be slightly shorter and stouter than average and to have later age at menopause. Hence, if the environment stays constant, these traits will presumably become more common over time because

The Viral Superhighway

By George J. Armelagos

Environmental disruptions and international travel have brought on a new era in human illness, one marked by diabolical new diseases.

So the Lord sent a pestilence upon Israel from the morning until the appointed time; and there died of the people from Dan to Beer-sheba seventy thousand men.
　　　　　　　　　　　　　—2 Sam. 24:15

Swarms of crop-destroying locusts, rivers fouled with blood, lion-headed horses breathing fire and sulfur: the Bible presents a lurid assortment of plagues, described as acts of retribution by a vengeful God. Indeed, real-life epidemics—such as the influenza outbreak of 1918, which killed 21 million people in a matter of months—can be so sudden and deadly that it is easy, even for nonbelievers, to view them as angry messages from the beyond.

How reassuring it was, then, when the march of technology began to give people some control over the scourges of the past. In the 1950s the Salk vaccine, and later, the Sabin vaccine, dramatically reduced the incidence of polio. And by 1980 a determined effort by health workers worldwide eradicated smallpox, a disease that had afflicted humankind since earliest times with blindness, disfigurement and death, killing nearly 300 million people in the twentieth century alone.

But those optimistic years in the second half of our century now seem, with hindsight, to have been an era of inflated expectations, even arrogance. In 1967 the surgeon general of the United States, William H. Stewart, announced that victory over infectious diseases was imminent—a victory that would close the book on modern plagues. Sadly, we now know differently. Not only have deadly and previously unimagined new illnesses such as AIDS and Legionnaires' disease emerged in recent years, but historical diseases that just a few decades ago seemed to have been tamed are returning in virulent, drug-resistant varieties. Tuberculosis, the ancient lung disease that haunted nineteenth-century Europe, afflicting, among others, Chopin. Dostoyevski and Keats, is aggressively mutating into strains that defy the standard medicines; as a result, modern TB victims must undergo a daily drug regimen so elaborate that health-department workers often have to personally monitor patients to make sure they comply [see "A Plague Returns," by Mark Earnest and John A. Sbarbaro, September/ October 1993]. Meanwhile, bacteria and viruses in foods from chicken to strawberries to alfalfa sprouts are sickening as many as 80 million Americans each year.

And those are only symptoms of a much more general threat. Deaths from infectious diseases in the United States rose 58 percent between 1980 and 1992. Twenty-nine new diseases have been reported in the new virus from central Africa infects unwitting Californians and starts an epidemic that threatens to annihilate the human race.

The reality about infectious disease is less sensational but alarming nonetheless. Gruesome new pathogens such as Ebola are unlikely to cause a widespread epidemic because they sicken and kill so quickly that victims can be easily identified and isolated; on the other hand, the seemingly innocuous practice of overprescribing antibiotics for bad colds could ultimately lead to untold deaths, as familiar germs evolve to become untreatable. We are living in the twilight of the antibiotic era: within our lifetimes, scraped knees and cut fingers may return to the realm of fatal conditions.

Through international travel, global commerce and the accelerating destruction of ecosystems worldwide, people are inadvertently exposing themselves to a Pandora's box of emerging microbial threats. And the recent rumblings of biological terrorism from Iraq highlight the appalling potential of disease organisms for being manipulated to vile ends. But although it may appear that the apocalypse has arrived, the truth is that people today are not facing a unique predicament. Emerging diseases have long loomed like a shadow over the human race.

People and pathogens have a long history together. Infections have been detected in the bones of human ancestors more than a million years old, and evidence from the mummy of the Egyptian pharaoh Ramses V suggests that he may have died from smallpox more than 3,000 years ago. Widespread outbreaks of disease are also well documented.

According to conventional wisdom in biology, people and invading microorganisms evolve together: people gradually become more resistant, and the microorganisms become less virulent. The result is either mutualism, in which the relation benefits both species, or commensalism, in which one species benefits without harming the other. Chicken pox and measles, once fatal afflictions, now exist in more benign forms. Logic would suggest, after all, that the best interests of an organism are not served if it kills its host; doing so would be like picking a fight with the person who signs your paycheck.

But recently it has become clear to epidemiologists that the reverse of that cooperative paradigm of illness can also be true: microorganisms and their hosts sometimes exhaust their energies devising increasingly powerful weaponry and defenses. For example, several variants of human immunodeficiency virus (HIV) may compete for dominance within a person's body, placing the immune system under ever-greater siege. As long as a virus has an effective mechanism for jumping from one person to another, it can afford to kill its victims [see "The Deadliest Virus," by Cynthia Mills, January/February 1997].

If the competition were merely a question of size, humans would surely win: the average person is 10^{17} times the size of the average bacterium. But human beings, after all, constitute only one species, which must compete with 5,000 kinds of viruses and more than 300,000 species of bacteria. Moreover, in the twenty years it takes humans to produce a new generation, bacteria can reproduce a half-million times. That disparity enables pathogens to evolve ever more virulent adaptations that quickly outstrip human responses to them. The scenario is governed by what the English zoologist Richard Dawkins of the University of Oxford and a colleague have called the "Red Queen Principle." In Lewis Carroll's *Through the Looking Glass* the Red Queen tells Alice she will need to run faster and faster just to stay in the same place. Staving off illness can be equally elusive.

The centers for disease control and Prevention (CDC) in Atlanta, Georgia, has compiled a list of the most recent emerging pathogens. They include:

- *Campylobacter,* a bacterium widely found in chickens because of the commercial practice of raising them in cramped, unhealthy conditions. It causes between two million and eight million cases of food poisoning a year in the United States and between 200 and 800 deaths.
- *Escherichia coli* 0157:H7, a dangerously mutated version of an often harmless bacterium. Hamburger meat from Jack in the Box fast-food restaurants that was contaminated with this bug led to the deaths of at least four people in 1993.
- Hantaviruses, a genus of fast-acting, lethal viruses, often carried by rodents, that kill by causing the capillaries to leak blood. A new hantavirus known as *sin nombre* (Spanish for "nameless") surfaced in 1993 in the southwestern United States, causing the sudden and mysterious deaths of thirty-two people.
- HIV, the deadly virus that causes AIDS (acquired immunodeficiency syndrome). Although it was first observed in people as recently as 1981, it has spread like wildfire and is now a global scourge, affecting more than 30 million people worldwide.
- The strange new infectious agent that causes bovine spongiform encephalopathy, or mad cow disease, which recently threw the British meat industry and consumers into a panic. This bizarre agent, known as a prion, or "proteinaceous infectious particle," is also responsible for Creutzfeldt-Jakob disease, the brain-eater I mentioned earlier. A Nobel Prize was awarded last year to the biochemist Stanley B. Prusiner of the University of California, San Francisco, for his discovery of the prion.
- *Legionella pneumophila,* the bacterium that causes Legionnaires' disease. The microorganism thrives in wet environments: when it lodges in air-conditioning systems or the mist machines in supermarket produce sections, it can be expelled into the air, reaching people's lungs. In 1976 thirty-four participants at an American Legion convention in Philadelphia died—the incident that led to the discovery and naming of the disease.
- *Borrelia burgdorferi,* the bacterium that causes Lyme disease. It is carried by ticks that live on deer and white-footed mice. Left untreated, it can cause crippling, chronic problems in the nerves, joints and internal organs.

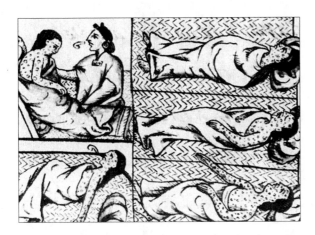

*Bernardino desahagun, smallpox epidemic in Mexico, (from **Historia de las cosas de Nueva Espana**), sixteenth century*

How ironic, given such a rogues' gallery of nasty characters, that just a quarter-century ago the Egyptian demographer Abdel R. Omran could observe that in many modern industrial nations the major killers were no longer infectious diseases. Death, he noted, now came not from outside but rather from within the body, the result of gradual deterioration. Omran traced the change to the middle of the nineteenth century, when the industrial revolution took hold in the United States and parts of Europe. Thanks to better nutrition, improved public-health measures implying as it did an end to the supremacy of microorganisms. Then, three years ago, I began working with the anthropologist Kathleen C. Barnes of Johns Hopkins University in Baltimore, Maryland, to formulate an expansion of Omran's ideas. It occurred to us that his epidemiological transition had not been a unique event. Throughout history human populations have undergone shifts in their relations with disease—shifts, we noted, that are always linked to major changes in the way people interact with the environment. Barnes and I, along with James Lin, a master's student at Johns Hopkins University School of Hygiene and Public Health, have since developed a new theory: that there have been not one but three major epidemiological transitions; that each one has been sparked by human activities: and that we are living through the third one right now.

The first epidemiological transition took place some 10,000 years ago, when people abandoned their nomadic existence and began farming. That profoundly new way of life disrupted ecosystems and created denser living conditions that led, as I will soon detail, to new diseases. The second epidemiological transition was the salutary one Omran singled out in 1971, when the war against infectious diseases seemed to have been won. And in the past two decades the emergence of illnesses such as hepatitis C, cat scratch disease (caused by the bacterium *Bartonella henselae),* Ebola and others on CDC's list has created a third epidemiological transition, a disheartening set of changes that in many ways have reversed the effects of the second transition and coincide with the shift to globalism. Burgeoning population growth and urbanization, widespread environmental degradation, including

earlier primates—included head and body lice; parasitic worms such as pinworms, tapeworms and liver flukes; and possibly herpes virus and malaria.

For 99.8 percent of the five million years of human existence, hunting and gathering was the primary mode of subsistence. Our ancestors lived in small groups and relied on wild animals and plants for their survival. In their foraging rounds, early humans would occasionally have contracted new kinds of illnesses through insect bites or by butchering and eating disease-ridden animals. Such events would not have led to widespread epidemics, however, because groups of people were so sparse and widely dispersed.

About 10,000 years ago, at the end of the last ice age, many groups began to abandon their nomadic lifestyles for a more efficient and secure way of life. The agricultural revolution first appeared in the Middle East; later, fanning centers developed independently in China and Central America. Permanent villages grew up, and people turned their attention to crafts such as toolmaking and pottery. Thus when people took to cultivating wheat and barley, they planted the seeds of civilization as well.

With the new ways, however, came certain costs. As wild habitats were transformed into urban settings, the fanners who brought in the harvest with their flint-bladed sickles were assailed by grim new ailments. Among the most common was scrub typhus, which is carried by mites that live in tall grasses, and causes a potentially lethal fever. Clearing vegetation to create arable fields brought fanners frequently into mite-infested terrain.

Irrigation brought further hazards. Standing thigh-deep in watery canals, farm workers were prey to the worms that cause schistosomiasis. After living within aquatic snails during their larval stage, those worms emerge in a tree-swimming form that can penetrate human skin, lodge in the intestine or urinary tract, and cause bloody urine and other serious maladies. Schistosomiasis was well known in ancient Egypt, where outlying fields were irrigated with water from the Nile River; descriptions of its symptoms and remedies are preserved in contemporary medical papyruses.

The domestication of sheep, goats and other animals cleared another pathway for microorganisms. With pigs in their yards and chickens roaming the streets, people in agricultural societies were constantly vulnerable to pathogens that could cross interspecies barriers. Many such organisms had long since reached commensalism with their animal hosts, but they were highly dangerous to humans. Milk from infected cattle could transmit tuberculosis, a slow killer that eats away at the lungs and causes its victims to cough blood and pus. Wool and skins were loaded with anthrax, which can be fatal when inhaled and, in modern times, has been developed by several nations as a potential agent of biological warfare. Blood from infected cattle, injected into people by biting insects such as the tsetse fly, spread sleeping sickness, an often-fatal disease marked by tremors and protracted lethargy.

A second major effect of agriculture was to spur population growth and, perhaps more important, density. Cities with populations as high as 50,000 had developed in the Near East by 3000 B.C. Scavenger species such as rats, mice and sparrows, which congregate wherever large groups of people live, exposed city dwellers to bubonic plague, typhus and rabies. And now that people were crowded together, a new pathogen could quickly start an epidemic. Larger populations also enabled diseases such as measles, mumps, chicken pox and smallpox to persist in an endemic form—always present, afflicting part of the population while sparing those with acquired immunity.

Thus the birth of agriculture launched humanity on a trajectory that has again and again brought people into contact with new pathogens. Tilling soil and raising livestock led to more energy-intensive ways of extracting resources from the earth—to lumbering, coal mining, oil drilling. New resources led to increasingly complex social organization, and to new and more frequent contacts between various societies. Loggers today who venture into the rain forest disturb previously untouched creatures and give them, for the first time, the chance to attack humans. But there is nothing new about this drama; only the players have changed. Some 2,000 years ago the introduction of iron tools to sub-Saharan Africa led to a slash-and-burn style of agriculture that brought people into contact with *Anopheles gambiae*, a mosquito that transmits malaria.

Improved transportation methods also help diseases extend their reach: microorganisms cannot travel far on their own, but they are expert hitchhikers. When the Spanish invaded Mexico in the early 1500s, for instance, they brought with them diseases that quickly raged through Tenochtitlan, the stately, temple-filled capital of the Aztec-Empire. Smallpox, measles and influenza wiped out millions of Central America's original inhabitants, becoming the invisible weapon in the European conquest.

In the past three decades people and their inventions have drilled, polluted, engineered, paved, planted and deforested at soaring rates, changing the biosphere faster than ever before. The combined effects can, without hyperbole, be called a global revolution. After all, many of them have worldwide repercussions: the widespread chemical contamination of waterways, the thinning of the ozone layer, the loss of species diversity.

And such global human actions have put people at risk for infectious diseases in newly complex and devastating ways. Global warming, for instance, could expose millions of people for the first time to malaria, sleeping sickness and other insect-borne illnesses; in the United States, a slight overall temperature increase would allow the mosquitoes that carry dengue fever to survive as far north as New York City.

Major changes to the landscape that have become possible in the past quarter-century have also a dominant factor in the emergence of Lyme disease—10,000 cases of which are reported annually. Thanks to modern earth-moving equipment, a soaring economy and population pressures, many Americans have built homes in formerly remote, wooded areas. Nourished by lawns and gardens and unchecked by wolves, which were exterminated by settlers long ago, the deer population has exploded, exposing people to the ticks that carry Lyme disease.

Meanwhile, widespread pollution has made the oceans a breeding ground for microorganisms. Epidemiologists have suggested that toxic algal blooms—fed by the sewage, fertilizers and other contaminants that wash into the oceans—harbor countless viruses and bacteria. Thrown together into what amounts to a dirty genetic soup, those pathogens can undergo gene-swapping and mutations, engendering newly antibiotic-resistant strains. Nautical traffic can carry ocean pathogens far and wide: a devastating outbreak of cholera hit Latin America in 1991 after a ship from Asia unloaded its contaminated ballast water into the harbor of Callao, Peru. Cholera causes diarrhea so severe its victims can die in a few days from dehydration: in that outbreak more than 300,000 people became ill, and more than 3,000 died.

The modern world is becoming—to paraphrase the words of the microbiologist Stephen S. Morse of Columbia University—a viral superhighway. Everyone is at risk.

Our newly global society is characterized by huge increases in population, international travel and international trade—factors that enable diseases to spread much more readily than ever before from person to person and from continent to continent.

tional borders each year on commercial flights. Not only does that traffic volume dramatically increase the chance a sick person will infect the inhabitants of a distant area when she reaches her destination; it also exposes the sick person's fellow passengers to the disease, because of poor air circulation on planes. Many of those passengers can, in turn, pass the disease on to others when they disembark.

The global economy that has arisen in the past two decades has established a myriad of connections between far-flung places. Not too long ago bananas and oranges were rare treats in northern climes. Now you can walk into your neighborhood market and find food that has been flown and trucked in from all over the world: oranges from Israel, apples from New Zealand, avocados from California. Consumers in affluent nations expect to be able to buy whatever they want whenever they want it. What people do not generally realize, however, is that this global network of food production and delivery provides countless pathways for pathogens. Raspberries from Guatemala, carrots from Peru and coconut milk from Thailand have been responsible for recent outbreaks of food poisoning in the United States. And the problem cuts both ways: contaminated radish seeds and frozen beef from the United States have ended up in Japan and South Korea.

Finally, the widespread and often indiscriminate use of antibiotics has played a key role in spurring disease. Forty million pounds of antibiotics are manufactured annually in the United States, an eightyfold increase since 1954. Dangerous microorganisms have evolved accordingly, often developing antibiotic-resistant strains. Physicians are now faced with penicillin-resistant gonorrhea, multiple-drug-resistant tuberculosis and *E. coli* variants such as 0157:H7. And frighteningly, some enterococcus bacteria have become resistant to *all* known antibiotics. Enterococcus infections are rare, but staphylococcus infections are not, and many strains of staph bacteria now respond to just one antibiotic, vancomycin. How long will it be before run-of-the-mill staph infections—in a boil, for instance, or in a surgical incision—become untreatable?

Although civilization can expose people to new pathogens, cultural progress also has an obvious countervailing effect: it can provide tools—medicines, sensible city planning, educational campaigns about sexually transmitted diseases—to fight the encroachments of disease. Moreover, since biology seems to side with microorganisms anyway, people have little choice but to depend on protective cultural practices to keep pace: vaccinations, for instance, to confer immunity, combined with practices such as hand-washing by physicians between patient visits, to limit contact between people and pathogens.

All too often, though, obvious protective measures such as using only clean hypodermic needles or treating urban drinking water with chlorine are neglected, whether out of ignorance or a wrong-headed emphasis on the short-term financial costs. The worldwide disparity in wealth is also to blame: not surprisingly, the advances made during the second epidemiological transition were limited largely to the affluent of the industrial world.

Such lapses are now beginning to teach the bitter lesson that the delicate balance between humans and invasive microorganisms can tip the other way again. Overconfidence—the legacy of the second epidemiological transition—has made us especially vulnerable to emerging and reemerging diseases. Evolutionary principles can provide this useful corrective: in spite of all our medical and technological hubris, there is no quick fix. If human beings are to overcome the current crisis, it will be through sensible changes in behavior, such as increased condom use and improved sanitation, combined with a commitment to stop disturbing the ecological balance of the planet.

The Bible, in short, was not far from wrong: We do bring plagues upon ourselves—not by sinning, but by refusing to heed our own alarms, our own best judgment. The price of peace—or at least peaceful coexistence—with the microorganisms on this planet is eternal vigilance.

GEORGE J. ARMELAGOS *is a professor of anthropology at Emory University in Atlanta, Georgia. He has coedited two books on the evolution of human disease:* PALEOPATHOLOGY AT THE ORIGINS OF AGRICULTURE, *which deals with prehistoric populations, and* DISEASE IN POPULATIONS IN TRANSITION, *which focuses on contemporary societies.*

Evolutionary, Historical and Political Economic Perspectives on Health and Disease

By George J. Armelagos, Peter J. Brown, and Bethany Turner

Abstract

The origin and rise of social inequalities that are a feature of the post-Neolithic society play a major role in the pattern of disease in prehistoric and contemporary populations. We use the concept of epidemiological transition to understand changing ecological relationships between humans, pathogens and other disease insults. With the Paleolithic period as a baseline, we begin with ecological and social relationships that minimized the impact of infectious disease. Paleolithic populations would have retained many of the pathogens that they shared with their primate ancestors and would have been exposed to zoonoses that they picked up as they adapted to a foraging existence. The sparse mobile populations would have precluded the existence of endemic infectious disease. About 10,000 years ago, the shift to an agricultural subsistence economy created the first epidemiological transition, marked by the emergence of infections, a pattern that has continued to the present. Beginning about a century ago, some populations have undergone a second epidemiological transition in which public health measures, improved nutrition and medicine resulted in declines in infectious disease and a rise in non-infectious, chronic and degenerative diseases. Human populations are entering the third epidemiological transition in which there is a reemergence of infectious diseases previously thought to be under control, and the emergence of novel diseases. Many of the emerging and reemerging pathogens are antibiotic resistant and some are multi-antibiotic resistant. Inequality continues to widen within and between societies, accelerating the spread of emerging and reemerging diseases. © 2004 Elsevier Ltd. All rights reserved.

Keywords: Epidemiological transition; Pathogen; Evolution; Social stratification

Introduction

The United States Surgeon General William T. Stewart, testifying before Congress in 1969, proclaimed that it was now ... time to close the book on infectious disease as a major health threat." Buoyed by the successful development of vaccines, antibiotics and pesticides, Stewart assumed that the eradication of infectious disease was imminent. Two years earlier, in a meeting with state medical officers Stewart claimed smallpox, bubonic plague, and malaria "were things of the past" and predicted (Ryan, 1997:6), typhoid, polio, and diphtheria were heading in the same direction. While syphilis, gonorrhea, and tuberculosis were not quite so readily defeated, it was only a matter of time before every

George J. Armelagos, Peter J. Brown, and Bethany Turner, "Evolutionary, historical and political economic perspectives on health and disease," from *Social Science & Medicine*, vol. 61; 2005, pp. 755–765. Copyright © 2005 by Elsevier. Permission to reprint granted by the publisher.

(WHO, 2001, Appendix A) reports that of the 55 million global deaths in the year 2000, 14 million were the result of infectious, parasitic and respiratory diseases. Nearly 4 million deaths due to lower respiratory infections were recorded; approximately 3 million deaths were attributed to HIV/ AIDS, over 2 million children succumbed to diarrheal disease, over a million and a half died from tuberculosis and 1 million deaths were from the consequences of malaria. The World Health Organization (WHO, 1995) calculates that 2 billion people in the world are infected with hepatitis B virus, two billion are infected with tuberculosis (Sizemore & Fauci, 2002) and 40 million people have AIDS (UNAIDS/WHO, 2001).

Stewart did not comprehend the degree to which antibiotic-resistant pathogens (Cassell & Mekalanos, 2001; Okeke & Edelman, 2001; van den Bogaard, & Stobberingh, 2000) and pesticide-resistant insects (Roberts & Andre, 1994) would become a problem, making the eradication of some disease vectors an impossibility. The extent of the impacts of ecological disruption (Mayer, 2000; Western, 2001; Woodruff, 2001) and of inequality (Houweling, Kunst, & Mackenbach, 2001; Wagstaff, 2000) on the disease process were also underestimated. *Homo sapiens* continue to create unprecedented ecological disturbances that are having unparalleled evolutionary impact (Palumbi, 2001). These ecological disturbances have accelerated changes in antibiotic and pesticide resistance and cost Americans an estimated 33 billion to 50 billion dollars a year (Palumbi, 2001).

The decline of infectious disease and the rise of chronic disease were thought to be the culmination modeled the transition of human populations from a state of pathogen-induced infections to a state of chronic, man-made disease (Omran, 1971:163). Omran's (1971, 1983) model was driven by processes that eliminated infectious diseases, allowing populations to age with a subsequent rise in chronic and degenerative diseases and those of "man's" making. Omran's use of the term "man-made" disease anticipated the contemporary roles that pollution and other by-products of the industrial age play in the disease process (Caldwell, 2001).

Our primary objective is to provide an evolutionary perspective on health and disease, using epidemiological transition to examine the role that wealth and poverty play in the process. Specifically, we are interested in the role that disparities in wealth (Brockerhoff & Hewett, 2000; Coburn, 2000; Hawe & Shiell, 2000; Shaw, Orford, Brimblecombe, & Dorling, 2000) play in continuing evolutionary processes that have affected humans for the last 500 generations. Social stratification originally evolved because it brought benefits to emerging elites. In general, these benefits, which often included resources that improved health, came at the expense of the others. We use the concept of macroparasitism (McNeill, 1976) to understand the changing pattern of inequality. When organisms appropriate others as continuing sources of food and energy, we can characterize that relationship as parasitism. Social stratification within societies and between them is an evolutionary strategy that we consider "macroparasitism"[1] (Brown, 1987; McNeill, 1976). We will discuss inequality in the changing relationships of pathogens and people as they experience epidemiological transitions.

Epidemiological Transition

Given the failure to eradicate infectious diseases or control emergent diseases, one might be tempted to reject the notion of epidemiological transitions. However, we are applying Omran's model in a broader evolutionary context. Armelagos and colleagues (Armelagos & Barnes, 1999; Barnes, Armelagos, & Morreale, 1999; Barrett, Kuzawa, McDade & Armelagos, 1998) have argued that human populations have gone through an earlier epidemiological transition and are presently experiencing a third.

The shift from foraging to primary food production represents the first epidemiological transition. The domestication of plants and animals in the Neolithic brought about a marked increase in the prevalence of infectious disease. Increase in population size and density, domestication of animals, sedentarism, cultivation and social stratification created a dramatic shift in disease ecology. Controversy surrounds the second epidemiological transition (Omran's original conceptualization). The causes and extents of the decline in infectious disease and the rise of chronic disease remain matters of debate. Finally, we are living in the third epidemiological transition in which many antibiotics are losing their effectiveness (Barrett et al., 1998). This period is characterized by the globalization of reemergent infectious diseases (Hughes, 2001; Morse, 1997) that are often resistant to multiple antibiotics (Farmer, 1997; Jacobs, 1994; Wellems & Plowe, 2001), and the emergence of novel diseases that threaten human populations.

We are well aware of the criticism of the concept of "emerging" disease. Paul Farmer (1996) argues that emerging diseases are only "discovered" when they have an impact on Americans. Lyme disease was an object of research years before wealthy suburbanites built houses in wooded golf course communities that change the ecology enough, creating an environment that brings ticks and rich humans together (Farmer, 1996). Furthermore, he claims that "emerging" diseases are usually presented as a result of human behavior or microbial changes. Even when researchers provide an ecological perspective for emerging disease, they will usually fail to consider them in a broader political-economic context (Farmer, 1996). It is precisely this criticism that we are addressing in the analysis of epidemiological transition presented here. We are interested in the social forces that influence inequality in an increasingly interconnected world, and how these inequalities affect the disease process (Farmer, 1996). Farmer's criticisms echo those made by Meredith Turshen (1977) a quarter of a century ago, in which she claims epidemiological models of that time focused narrowly on relationships between hosts, pathogens and the environment and failed to consider the cultural, political and economic complexity in the disease process.

With economic and technological development, there has been an evolutionary tendency for the disparities between the rich and the poor, the healthy and the sick, to increase. In this century, the widening gap between those on the top and the bottom of the social hierarchy occurs both within and between societies (Houweling et al., 2001; Shaw et al., 2000), and is greater than ever before in human history. This gap has serious health implications. While disease and death are inevitable, a major cause of unnecessary, premature, preventable disease and death is simple; it is extreme poverty.

---

[1] It is interesting to note that parasitism originally referred to a human social relationship. According to the *Oxford English Dictionary*, parasitism was defined by the ancient Greeks as a relationship in which a wealthy patron would pay a person to dine with and entertain him. The earliest English recording of the world continues this usage. Beginning from 1727-1741, parasite described biological pathogenesis and then was restricted to botanical relationships.

staphylococci (Cockburn, 1967a, b) are examples of heirloom pathogens.

Zoonoses are souvenir species (Sprent, 1962, 1969) whose primary hosts are non-human animals, and who only incidentally infect humans. Insect bites, processing and eating contaminated meat, and animal bites are sources of zoonotic disease. Avian or ichthyic tuberculosis, leptospirosis, relapsing fever, schistosomiasis, scrub typhus, tetanus, trichinoses, trypanosomiasis and tetanus are among the zoonotic diseases that likely afflicted earlier gatherer-hunters (Cockburn, 1971). However, small population sizes would have precluded infectious diseases having a major evolutionary impact and the daily forays of gatherer-hunters from their base camps and frequent movement of these camps would have decreased their contact with parasites found in human feces. Deadly diseases would soon run their course as the small number of susceptible individuals was infected. Paleolithic populations lacked the common and deadly communicable diseases such as influenza, measles, mumps, and smallpox.

Gatherer-hunters are equal opportunity hosts. Because of their egalitarian nature, they lack the class structure that creates differential exposure to disease among segments of the society. However, as women gather and men hunt (the producing segment of society), they are differentially exposed to disease vectors in the course of their daily subsistence rounds. While men may be exposed to pathogens and parasites as they prepare the animals they kill, women cooking the meat would be similarly exposed. Since the producing segments of the society are differentially infected, diseases may have a more disruptive effect on the survival of the group.

crease in population size and density, sedentarism, the domestication of animals, extensive ecological disruption from cultivation and the rise of social and economic inequality are all factors that increase infectious disease risk.

By 5000 BCE, large settlements existed in Mesopotamia, and 1000 years later, the rise of centralized polities that controlled vast irrigation systems are evident. In Mexico, by 3500 years ago, well-established settlements arose with evidence of extensive hierarchies rising 1500 years later. The political and economic changes with the development of agriculture created social classes with differential access to resources, a system that continues to this day.

Sedentarism increased parasitic infection because of proximity of the living areas to source of waters and the areas where human waste was deposited. The contiguity of habitation to the space where domesticated animals were kept, created a cluster of disease vectors. Parasites, such as tapeworms associated with domesticated goats, sheep, cattle, pigs, and fowl, would have infected these early farmers. However, recent research on the tapeworm's *(Taenia)* genetic phylogeny (Hoberg, Jones, Rausch, Eom, & Gardner, 2000) suggests that the differentiation among the common parasites occurred during the Paleolithic and that humans were the source of infections in cattle, sheep and goats that occurred after domestication of these species.

The milk, hair, and skin of domesticates, as well as animal dust, transmitted anthrax, Q fever, brucellosis, and tuberculosis. Peridomestic animals such as rodents and sparrows, which are drawn to human habitats, are also a source of disease. Cultivation often exposes workers to insect bites, and diseases such as scrub typhus becomes common (Audy, 1961). Livingstone (1958) and Wiesenfeld (1967) show that slash-and-burn agriculture in West Africa exposed populations to the mosquito that is the vector for malaria. Environmental disturbances during the clearing and cultivating of land increase human contact with arthropod vectors that prefer human habitats and that carry yellow fever and filariasis. For example, *Aedes aegypti* (the vector for yellow fever and dengue) is an artificial container breeder. Irrigation agriculture (Sattenspiel, 2000; Watts, Khallaayoune, Bensefia, Laamrani, & Gryseels, 1998) and fertilizing with human waste increases contact with non-vector parasites (Cockburn, 1971).

Surprisingly, agriculture subsistence increased dietary deficiencies that had health implication for agriculturalists after the Neolithic (Cohen & Armelagos, 1984). Agricultural subsistence invariably reduces the variety of foods that are available to people (Armelagos, 1987) and many increase a reliance on a single-grain crop such a millet, rice, wheat or maize. The reduction of the dietary niche (Katz, 1987) resulted in dietary deficiencies that can increase the impact of infectious disease (Guerrant, Lima, & Davidson, 2000; Rice, Sacco, Hyder, & Black, 2000; Stephenson, Latham, & Ottesen, 2000) while food storage increased the potential for food poisoning (Brothwell & Brothwell, 1998). The combination of a complex society, increasing divisions of class, epidemic disease, and dietary insufficiencies increases the stress levels in the population.

Paynter (1989) suggests that social stratification may not have initially reflected inequality. Even though the distinctions between rulers and ruled may have been great, there may be equality within the ruled group. Nevertheless, research on Middle Mississippian populations (Goodman, Lallo, Armelagos, & Rose, 1984)—well-defined chiefdoms—suggests that those populations were suffering from significant nutritional and infectious disease stress.

Urban Development and Disease During the Neolithic

The impact of contemporary urbanization on health has been studied extensively (Lawrence, 1999; McMichael, 2000). Large settlements increased the already difficult problem of removing human wastes and delivering uncontaminated water. Cholera, a waterborne disease, became a potential problem and lice that carried typhus and the fleas infested with the plague bacillus spread disease from person to person. High population densities enhanced the respiratory transmission of the plague and the transmission of viral diseases such as measles, mumps, chicken pox, and smallpox.

The rapid urbanization of human populations and expansion into new ecological zones represents one of the most important forces in the evolution of infectious disease. From their earliest beginnings, urban centers established in the Near East and in the western hemisphere grew rapidly. Urban centers at Memphis (Egypt) reached 30,000 individuals by 3100 BCE, Ur in Babylonia reached 65,000 inhabitants by 2030 BCE and Babylon had a population of 200,000 by 612 BCE (Chandler, 1987). Populations of this size could maintain some diseases in an endemic form. For example, estimates of the population size necessary to maintain measles vary from 200,000 (Black et al., 1974) to 1,000,000 people (Cockburn, 1967a).

The processes of urbanization and globalization (Robertson, 1992), and the era of exploration in the fifteenth and sixteenth centuries were linked. McNeill (1976) describes the confluence of civilizations in Eurasia (500 BCE-1200 CE) and the development of the Mongol Empire (1200-1500 CE), which created a unique disease pool where pathogens are shared over a large area. Earlier trade in the Old World and exploration in the fifteenth and sixteenth centuries made inevitable transcontinental and transoceanic disease exchange that increased the potential for an endemic disease to be transmitted as epidemic disease in areas of contact.

Cross-continental trade and travel resulted in intense epidemics (McNeill, 1976; Zinsser, 1935). The plague, which was an endemic disease in China, mid villages abandoned in aftermath of ravaging diseases (Dobyns, 1983; Ramenofsky, 1987).

The transmission of disease is usually a two-way street. Since the Americas never had the collection of domesticated animals characteristic of the Old World Neolithic, they did not have a large variety of endemic zoonoses that could easily be transmitted to the Europeans. However, it is likely that the New World was the source of the treponemal infection transmitted to Europe. The Native Americans had an endemic non-venereal treponemal infection (Rothschild, Calderon, Coppa, & Rothschild, 2000) that was transmitted to the Old World (Baker & Armelagos, 1988). When introduced into the Old World, the sexual transmission of the treponeme resulted in a more severe and acute infection. Counterclaims that pre-Columbian syphilis existed in Europe have been made (Dutour, Palfi, Berato, & Brun, 1994), but the resolution of this debate may await the recovery of material that can be identified as a treponemal pathogen from Old World, pre-Columbian archaeological bone.

Urbanization in a Industrial World

The process of industrialization, which began a little over 200 years ago, led to an even greater environmental and social transformation. In 1800, London was the only city in the world with a million inhabitants. City dwellers would have been forced to contend with industrial wastes and polluted water and air. Slums that rose in industrial cities would become the focal point for poverty and the spread of disease. Epidemics of smallpox, drew migrants to the squalor of the cities that were "population sinks".

In 1800, when London was the only city of a million people, just 3% of the world's population lived in an urban setting. By 1900, urban dwellers had increased to 14%, with 12 cities having a million or more inhabitants. Fifty years later (1950) this proportion had increased to 30%. Now, about 47% of the population lives in urban areas, and the number of cities with over a million inhabitants has risen to 411 (United Nations, 2000). In the developed nations, the percent of urbanites has reached 76%—nearly twice the proportion of developing nations. The projected increase for the year 2030 is that 60% of the world's population will be living in urban centers and that this increase will occur in the less developed nations (United Nations, 2002) which lack the infrastructure to meet the health needs of urban population (Garrett, 1994, 2001).

In 1950, New York City with a population 12 million was the largest megacity (populations over 5 million) in the world, and at that time, only two of the largest top 10 urban agglomerates were in developing countries. At the beginning of this century, six of the largest urban areas (all with over 12 million inhabitants) were in developing countries, and it is projected that by 2015, there will be eight centers, all with over 17 million inhabitants, in the same category, four of which will be on the Indian subcontinent.

The detrimental effects of industrialization have continued globally as pollution from the industrial production of commodities has created health concerns (The American Lung Association, 2001). The implications of contaminated water, pesticide use and depleted ozone on human health and food production are significant, for at no other periods in human history have the changes in the environment been so rapid and so extreme. Consequently, WHO has made the health problems of cities one of its major initiatives (Goldstein, 2000; Harpham, Burton, & Blue, 2001; Kenzer, 2000; McMichael, 2000; Tsouros, 2000).

The Second Epidemiological Transition: The Rise of Chronic and Degenerative Disease

The increasing prevalence of chronic diseases is related to increases in lifespan longevity that have occurred over the past few centuries. Cultural advances have resulted in a larger percentage of individuals reaching the oldest age segment of the population, while the technological advances that characterize the second epidemiological transition often result in an increase in environmental degradation.

The development of the germ theory of disease has been considered as the major force behind the decline of some infectious diseases. However, others have noted infectious diseases were declining before the initiation of many immunization programs and therapeutic practices (McKeown, 1979). Critics of McKeown have focused on his use of evidence for improved nutrition (Johansson, 1992; Schofield & Reher, 1991) and failure to consider improvements in public health practices (Johansson, 1992; Kunitz, 1991; Schofield & Reher, 1991). The development of immunization resulted in the control of many infections and was the primary factor in the recent eradication of smallpox; as well, in developed nations, a number of other communicable diseases have diminished in importance. The decrease in infectious diseases and the subsequent reduction in infant mortality have resulted in greater life expectancies at birth; the resulting increase in elderly individuals has yielded an increase in chronic and degenerative diseases.

At another level, critics argue that many countries have never experienced the second epidemiological

transition and in others, the transformation varied (Barrett et al., 1998). Since the 1960s, in some countries the rate of the decline in infectious disease has decelerated (Gwatkin, 1980), never reaching the levels in the developing world (Gobalet, 1989). Rapid urbanization, marked social inequalities and a lack of public health infrastructure have resulted in the pattern where the poorest segments of the population are exposed to infectious diseases, while chronic degenerative diseases have increased among the affluent and emerging middle classes (Muktatkar, 1995). In Mexico and Brazil and other middle-income countries, socioeconomic status is inversely related to risk of chronic diseases (Popkin, 1994). This pattern is similar to what we see in affluent nations such as the United States and the United Kingdom (Kaplan & Keil, 1993). This differential impact within and between nations reflects the influences of economic factors on the disease process. We have never considered epidemiological theory as a unilinear evolutionary model, and the variation others see as problematic, we see as an object of further study.

The Third Epidemiological Transition

Human populations are in the midst of the third epidemiological transition, in which there is a reemergence of infectious diseases, many of which are multiple antibiotic resistant, and have a great potential for global impact. In this sense, the contemporary transition does not eliminate the possible co-existence of infectious diseases typical of the first epidemiological transition (some 10,000 years ago) and degenerative disease of the second.

The reemergence of infectious diseases has been one of the most interesting evolutionary stories of the last decade, capturing the interest of scientists and the public (Drexler, 2002). A list of the 29 most recent emerging diseases has been reported in the last three decades (Lederberg, 1998; Lederberg, Shope, & Oaks, 1992), citing these as the result of an interaction of social, demographic and environmental changes in global ecology and in the adaptation and genetics of microbes. Morse (1995) sees emerging has been a factor in the spread of dengue (which is now becoming an urban disease), as well as the source for the introduction and spread of HIV and other sexually transmitted diseases.

The forces that generate the reemergence of many of these diseases are the ecological change that brings humans into contact with pathogens. Except for the Brazilian pururic fever, which may represent a new strain of *Haemophilus influenzae, Biotype aegyptius,* most of the emerging diseases are anthropogenic. The role of humans in the development of antibiotic resistance by way of medical and agricultural practices is a deadly example of human impact on pathogenic evolution.

Conclusion: Current Inequality and Health

We have provided an evolutionary perspective for understanding the emergence of disease since the Neolithic. Furthermore, inequalities between and within societies, which increase the risk for contracting infectious diseases that began in the Neolithic, have widened. In the United States from 1947 to 1979, all economic levels experienced three decades of improved prosperity (Table 1). The bottom 80% of American families experienced improvements of income of at least 100%. The top 20% showed 99% growth and the top 5% with the highest family income realized an 86% increase. But from 1979 to 1998, there occurred a remarkable economic decline for the families in the lower economic range. The poorest 20% of families actually suffered a 5% decline in family income. The second quintile improved 3%, the middle quintile gained

60% of the population in the middle experienced a nearly 65% decline in wealth. This disparity is reflected in The World Bank's Gini coefficient. A coefficient of zero would indicate equal distribution of income and a coefficient of one would indicate that all the income is in the hands of one individual or group. The Gini index has increased globally from .54 to .70 in the last 40 years.

Table 1 Rising together and drifting apart. Changes in family income from 1947 to 1979 and 1979 to 1998 by quintile and top 5%. Parentheses in the drifting apart column represents after taxes income

	Rising together (%)	Drifting apart (%)
	1947-1979	1979-1998
Top 5%	86	64 (115)
Top 20%	99	38 (43)
Fourth 20%	114	15 (14)
Middle 20%	111	8 (8)
Second 20%	100	3 (1)
Bottom 20%	116	-5(-9)

Source: 1947-1979: Analysis of US Census Bureau data in Economic Policy Institute, The State of Working America 1994-1995, p. 37. 1979-1998: US Census Bureau, Historical Income Tables, Table F-3. The after taxes data is from Center on Budget and Policy Priorities, The Widening Income Gulf, September 4, 1999.

Table 2 Growing global disparity

	1960 (%)	1970 (%)	1980 (%)	1989 (%)	1998 (%)
Highest 20%	70.2	73.9	76.3	82.7	89.0
Middle 60%	27.5	23.6	22.0	15.9	9.8
Lowest 20%	2.3	2.3	1.7	1.4	1.2
Gini	.54	.57	.60	.65	.70

Source: United Nations Development Program 1996. Extracted by poorcity.richcity.com/entundp.htm.

To put this inequality in another perspective, the 200 richest people in the world have a combined wealth equivalent to the wealth of 2.5 billion of the poorest people. Three Americans (Bill Gates, Paul Allen and Warren Buffett) have personal wealth greater that the GDP (Gross Domestic Products) of the world's 41 poorest nations and their 550 million citizens (Gates, 2000:6). In terms of health, 968 million people in developing nations are without access to safe water, 2.4 billion lack basic sanitation, 163 million children under 5 years of age are underweight and 11 million children die each year from preventable diseases (UNDP, 2001).

However, we have to address an ongoing debate in the social sciences centered on the relationship, if any, between economic inequalities, characterized chiefly by differential incomes, and health outcomes. R.G. Wilkinson (1998) is well known as an outspoken proponent of the notion that income inequality is a driving force in the creation of class discrimination and both external and internal value judgments based on one's position in an economically based social hierarchy (Wilkinson, 1999). Describing statistically robust correlations between the level of income inequality in and between societies and differential health outcomes, Wilkinson has shown that wealthier individuals tend to be healthier than those who are poorer. Such a hypothesis is supported when relative income differences are linked to levels of social solidarity and relative egalitarianism (Egolf, Lasker, Wolf, & Potvin, 1992), and when placed in the larger context of globalization (Coburn, 2000; McMichael, 2000). Recently, critics such as Deaton

(2001) have rejected Wilkinson's hypothesis that relative income inequality impacts health, emphasizing impoverishment and social discrimination as more important variables than income. Yet Deaton's critique holds only if one looks at income as a static and exclusive category, a theoretical perspective that does not seem particularly useful. To say that political inequality and income inequality are separate things (Deaton, 2001, 24), especially in a capitalist system such as Britain or the United States, ignores their interconnectivity and the effects that racism and sexism can have on job opportunities and thus income. Montague (1996) corroborates Wilkinson's statements that morbidity and mortality are higher amongst the poor than the rich, and agrees that it is not the average income of a society that is the most important indicator, but the size of the gap between the richest and the poorest in a society. This conclusion has been observed at international levels (Syme, 2000) and is supported within the historical and evolutionary frameworks of this paper.

Global capitalism as an economic strategy (macro-parasitism) has allowed members of the so-called 'First World' to accumulate vast quantities of material and social capital, often through the large-scale exploitation of resources and people in the 'Third World'. The social power gained by elites can insulate them from food shortages and unhygienic living conditions endured by the poor, which are in part due to the actions of elites (Gardner & Halweil, 2000).

An additional aspect of the macroparasitic strategy is ideological in its attribution of causality regarding global inequity and health. Blame is often assigned to outside entities such as genes, miasma or germs, or else to the moral inadequacy of individuals in failing to raise themselves up out of their situation. Diseases such as AIDS and leprosy are often attributed to the unsavory behavior or lack of moral fiber of the victims (Farmer, 1996), rather than to the statistical vulnerability and chronic misery of being poor. This allows elite classes to present themselves as superior in both biological and ideological spheres, obscuring the role that they play in causing, exacerbating and perpetuating the problem of global inequality and widespread poverty.

water. In these countries, factors such as resource scarcity, inadequate education and pollution must be addressed before any permanent solutions can be reached (United Nations, 2000).

Max Weber's definition of social class hinged on the notion of differential "life chances". Health indicators of morbidity, mortality and life expectancy are therefore appropriate measures of "life chances" that vary inversely with wealth. The concept of "life chances" supports the notion that poverty is, at its core, a reduction in or elimination of choices, as well as access to strategic resources such as food, clean water, medicine, land, money, education and social mobility. Gardner and Halweil (2000) attribute much of the plight of the poor not to shortages, but to the unequal distribution of wealth and the concentration of resources in a privileged global minority. They see the origins of this asymmetry in the political and economic decisions of the late 20th century such as the support of agribusiness and "trickle-down" economics, and the failure to support the efforts of independent farms and businesses in both the First and "developing" Third Worlds. Echoing these statements is a quote from the British Medical Journal (1996), which reads, "What matters in determining mortality and health in a society is less the overall wealth of that society and more how evenly wealth is distributed. The more equally wealth is distributed, the better the health of society."

The world's biggest killer and greatest cause of ill health and suffering across the globe is listed almost at the end of the International Classification of Disease (ICD). It is given in code Z59.5—extreme poverty. Of course, with this WHO ICD classification there is the question: what is *extreme* poverty?

for investments in public health" for the past 60 years. The implication is that a public health intervention would reverse this into an upward spiral of health and wealth; an example is the "malaria blocks development model" (Brown, 1997). Recently, Sachs and colleagues (Gallup & Sachs, 2001, Sachs & Malaney, 2002, Sachs, 2001) have demonstrated again on the level of cross-national data, that diseases like malaria carry a heavy economic burden that limit the possibility of economic growth in malaria-prone nations.

These issues are at the core of medical anthropology in its most ancient beginnings, and it is impossible to understand current issues of inequality without examining their historical roots. It is also necessary to examine the rise of chronic and epidemic diseases, nutritional stress and social inequalities as inextricably linked as we have done in this paper. It is hoped that based on conclusions here, others will take this multifaceted and evolutionary approach, addressing epidemiology, nutrition, poverty and globalization, in order to gain the level of understanding necessary to begin to address these problems. Rudolf Virchow in 1849 (Die Einheitsbestre-bungen) argued, "Once medicine is established as anthropology, and once the interests of the privileged no longer determine the course of public events, the physiologist and the practitioner will be counted among the elder statesmen who support the social structure. Medicine is a social science in its very bone and marrow." (Virchow 1958)

References

American Lung Association (2001). Urban air pollution and health inequities: a workshop report. *Environmental Health Perspectives,* 109(Suppl 3), 357-374.

Armelagos, G. J. (1987). Biocultural aspects of food choice. In Harris, M., & Ross, E. (Eds.), *Food and evolution* (pp. 579-594). Philadelphia: Temple University Press.

Armelagos, G. J., & Barnes, K. (1999). The evolution of human disease and the rise of allergy: epidemiological transitions. *Medical Anthropology, 18,* 187-213.

Audy, J. R. (1961). The ecology of scrub typhus. In May, J. M. (Ed.), *Studies in disease ecology* (pp. 389-432). New York: Hafner Publishing.

Baker, B., & Armelagos, G. J. (1988). Origin and antiquity of syphilis: a dilemma in paleopathological diagnosis and interpretation. *Current Anthropology, 29,* 703-737.

Barnes, K. C., Armelagos, G. J., & Morreale, S. C. (1999). Darwinian medicine and the emergence of allergy. In Trevethan, W., McKenna, J., & Smith, E. O. (Eds.), *Evolutionary medicine.* New York: Oxford University Press.

Barrett, R., Kuzawa, C. W., McDade, T., & Armelagos, G. J. (1998). Emerging infectious disease and the third epidemio-logical transition. In Durham, W. (Ed.), *Annual Review Anthropology* (pp. 247-271). Palo Alto, LA: Annual Reviews Inc.

Black, F. L., Hierholzer, W. J., Pinheiro, F., Evans, A. S., Woodall, J. P., Opton, E. M., et al. (1974). Evidence for persistence of infectious agents in isolated human populations. *American Journal of Epidemiology, 100,* 230-250.

British Medical Journal (1996). Editor's choice: the big idea. BMJ, *312* (April 20). www.bmj.bmjjournals.com/cgi/con-tent/full/312/7037.

Brockerhoff, M., & Hewett, P. (2000). Inequality of child mortality among ethnic groups in sub-Saharan Africa. *Bulletin of the World Health Organization, 78,* 30-41.

Brothwell, D. R., & Brothwell, P. (1998). *Food in antiquity: a survey of the diet of early peoples.* Baltimore, Md: Johns Hopkins University Press.

Brown, P. J. (1987). Microparasites and macroparasites. *Cultural Anthropology, 2,* 155-171.

Brown, P. J. (1997). Malaria, miseria, and under population in Sardinia: the "malăria blocks development" cultural model. *Medical Anthropology, 17,* 239-254.

Caldwell, J. C. (2001). Population health in transition. *Bulletin of the World Health Organization, 79,* 159-160.

Cassell, G. H., & Mekalanos, J. (2001). Development of antimicrobial agents in the era of new and reemerging infectious diseases and increasing antibiotic resistance. *Journal of the American Medical Association, 285,* 601-605.

Chandler, T. (1987). *Four thousand years of urban growth: an historical census.* Lewiston, N.Y.: Edward Mellen Press.

Coburn, D. (2000). Income inequality, social cohesion and the health status of populations: the role of neo-liberalism. *Social Science & Medicine, 51,* 135-146.

Cockburn, T. A. (1967a). The evolution of human infectious diseases. In Cockburn, T. A. (Ed.), *Infectious diseases: their evolution and eradication* (pp. 84-107). Springfield, IL: Charles C. Thomas.

Cockburn, T. A. (1967b). Infections of the order primates. In Cockburn, T. A. (Ed.), *Infectious diseases: their evolution and eradication.* Springfield, IL: Charles C. Thomas.

Cockburn, T. A. (1971). Infectious disease in ancient populations. *Current Anthropology, 12,* 45-62.

Cohen, M. N., & Armelagos, G. J. (Eds.). (1984). *Paleopathology at the origins of agriculture.* New York: Academic Press.

Deaton, A., (2001). *Relative deprivation, inequality and mortality.* Working Paper 8099, National Bureau of Economic Research, Inc, Cambridge, Massachusetts.

Dobyns, H. (1983). *Their numbers become thinned: native american population dynamics in eastern United States.* Knoxville: University of Tennessee Press.

Drexler, M. (2002). *Secret agents: The menace of emerging disease.* Washington DC: John Henry Press.

Dutour, O., Palfi, G., Berato, J., & Brun, J.-P. (1994). *L'origine de la Syphilis en Europe—Avant ou Apres 1493?.* Paris: Errance.

Medicine & Hygiene,64, 85-96.

Gardner, G. T., & Halweil, B. (2000). Underfed and overfed: the global epidemic of malnutrition. In Peterson, J. A. (Ed.), *Worldwatch paper 150.* Washington DC: Worldwatch Institute.

Garrett, L. (1994). *The coming plague: newly emerging diseases in world out of balance.* New York: Farrar Straus and Giroux.

Garrett, L. (2001). *Betrayal of trust: the collapse of global public health.* New York: Hyperion. Gates, J. (2000). Free talk on free trade. *Monthly Review* March 2000.

Gobalet, J. C. (1989). *World mortality trends since 1870.* New York: Garland.

Goldstein, G. (2000). Healthy cities: overview of a WHO international program. *Reviews on Environmental Health,* 15, 207-214.

Goodman, A. H., Lallo, J., Armelagos, G. J., & Rose, J. C. (1984). Health changes at Dickson Mounds (A.D. 950-1300). In Cohen, M. N., & Armelagos, G. J. (Eds.), *Paleopathology at the origins of agriculture* (pp. 271-305). Orlando, Florida: Academic Press. Gottfried, R. (1983). *The black death.* New York: Free Press.

Guerrant, R. L., Lima, A. A., & Davidson, F. (2000). Micronutrients and infection: interactions and implications with enteric and other infections and future priorities. *Journal of Infectious Diseases,* 182(Suppl 1), S134-S138.

Gwatkin, D. R. (1980). Indications of change in developing country mortality trends: the end of an era? *Population and Development Review, 33,* 615-644.

Harpham, T., Burton, S., & Blue, I. (2001). Healthy city projects in developing countries: the first

index and socioeconomic inequalities in mortality. *Lancet, 357,* 1671-1672.

Hughes, J.M., (2001). Emerging infectious diseases: a CDC perspective. *Emerging Infectious Diseases, 7.*

Jacobs, R. F. (1994). Multiple-drug-resistant tuberculosis. *Clinical Infectious Diseases, 19,* 1-8.

Johansson, S. R. (1992). Measuring the cultural inflation of morbidity during the decline in mortality. *Health Transition Review, 2,* 78-89.

Kaplan, G. A., & Keil, J. E. (1993). Socioeconomic factors and cardiovascular disease: a review of the literature. *Circula-tion\Circulation (New York), 88,* 1973-1998.

Katz, S. H. (1987). Food and biocultural evolution: A model for the Investigation of modern nutritional problems. In Johnston, F. E. (Ed.), *Nutritional Anthropology* (pp. 41-63). New York: Alan R. Liss, Inc.

Kenzer, M. (2000). Healthy Cities: a guide to the literature. *Public Health Reports, 115,* 279-289.

Kunitz, S. J. (1991). The personal physician and the decline of mortality. In Sclofield, D. R. R., & Bideau, A. (Eds.), *The decline of mortality in Europe* (pp. 248-262). Oxford: Clarendon Press.

Lawrence, R. J. (1999). Urban health: an ecological perspective. *Reviews on Environmental Health, 14,* 1-10.

Lederberg, J. (1998). Emerging infections: an evolutionary perspective. *Emerging Infectious Diseases, 4,* 366-371.

Lederberg, J., Shope, R. E., & Oaks, S. C. (Eds.). (1992). *Emerging Infection: microbial threats to health in the United States.* Institute of Medicine: National Academy Press.

Livingstone, F. B. (1958). Anthropological implications of sickle-cell distribution in West Africa. *American Anthropologist, 60*, 533-562.

Mayer, J. D. (2000). Geography, ecology and emerging infectious diseases. *Social Science & Medicine, 50*, 937-952.

McKeown, T. (1979). *The role of medicine: dream, mirage or nemesis.* Princeton: Princeton University Press.

McMichael, A. J. (2000). The urban environment and health in a world of increasing globalization: issues for developing countries. *Bulletin of the World Health Organization, 78*, 1117-1126.

McNeill, W. H. (1976). *Plagues and people.* Garden City: Anchor/Doubleday.

McNeill, W. H. (1978). Disease in history. *Social Science &*

Medicine, 12, 79-81. Montague, P. (1996). Economic inequality and health. *Racheal's Environment and Health Weekly, 497,* June 6. Morse, S. S. (1995). Factors in the emergence of infectious diseases. *Emerging Infectious Diseases, 1,* 7-15.

Morse, S. S. (1997). The public health threat of emerging viral disease. *Journal of Nutrition, 127,* 951S-957S.

Muktatkar, R. (1995). Public health problems of urbanization. *Social Science & Medicine, 41,* 977-981.

Okeke, I. N., & Edelman, R. (2001). Dissemination of antibiotic-resistant bacteria across geographic borders. *Clinical Infectious Diseases, 33,* 364-369.

Omran, A. R. (1971). The epidemiologic transition: a theory of the epidemiology of population change. *Millbank Memorial Fund Quarterly, 49,* 509-538.

Omran, A. R. (1983). The epidemiologic transition theory: a preliminary update. *Journal of Tropical Pediatrics, 29,* 305-316.

Palumbi, S. R. (2001). Humans as the world's greatest evolutionary force. *Science, 293,* 1786-1790.

Paynter, R. (1989). The archaeology of equality. *Annual Review of Anthropology, 18,* 369-399.

Polgar, S. (1964). Evolution and the ills of mankind. In Tax, S. (Ed.), *Horizons of anthropology* (pp. 200-211). Chicago: Aldine Publishing Company.

Popkin, B. M. (1994). The nutrition transition in low-income countries: an emerging crisis. *Nutrition Reviews, 52,* 285-298.

Ramenofsky, A. F. (1987). *Vectors of death: the archaeology of European contact.* Albuquerque, NM: University of New Mexico Press in association with the Center for Documentary Studies at Duke University.

Rice, A. L., Sacco, L., Hyder, A., & Black, R. E. (2000). Malnutrition as an underlying cause of childhood deaths associated with infectious diseases in developing countries. *Bulletin of the World Health Organization, 78,* 1207-1221.

Roberts, D. R., & Andre, R. G. (1994). Insecticide resistance issues in vector-borne disease control. *American Journal of Tropical Medicine & Hygiene, 50,* 21-34. Robertson, R. (1992). *Globalization: social theory and global culture.* London: Sage.

Rothschild, B. M., Calderon, F. L., Coppa, A., & Rothschild, C. (2000). First European exposure to syphilis: the Dominican Republic at the time of Columbian contact. *clinical Infectious Diseases, 31,* 936-941.

Ryan, F. (1997). *Virus X: Tracking the new killer plagues: out of the present into the future.* Boston: Little Brown.

Sachs, J. D. (2001). A new global commitment to disease control in Africa. *Nature Medicine, 7,* 521-523 [see comments].

Sachs, J., & Malaney, P. (2002). The economic and social burden of malaria. *Nature, 415,* 680-685.

Sattenspiel, L., (2000). Tropical environments, human activities, and the transmission of infectious diseases. *American Journal of Physical Anthropology, Suppl31,* 3-31.

Schofield, R., & Reher, D. (1991). The decline of mortality in Europe. In Schofield, R., Reher, D., & Bideau, A. (Eds.), *The decline of mortality in Europe* (pp. 1-17). Oxford: Claredon Press.

Shaw, M., Orford, S., Brimblecombe, N., & Dorling, D. (2000). Widening inequality in mortality between 160 regions of 15 European countries in the early 1990s. *Social Science & Medicine, 50,* 1047-1058.

Sizemore, C., & Fauci, A. S. (2002). *World TB day, March 24, 2002.* Washington: National Institute of Allergy and Infectious Disease.

Sprent, J. F. A. (1962). Parasitism, immunity and evolution. In Leeper, G. S. (Ed.), *The evolution of living organisms* (pp. 149-165). Melbourne: Melbourne University Press.

nored: the way forward. *Reviews on Environmental Health, 15*, 267-271.

Turshen, M. (1977). The political ecology of disease. *The Review of Radical Political Economics, 9*, 45-60.

UNAIDS/WHO (2001). *Aids epidemic update, December 2001*. Geneva: Joint United Nations Programme on HIV/AIDS (UNAIDS) and World Health Organization (WHO).

UNDP (2001). *Human development report 2001*. New York: Oxford University Press. United Nations (2000). *World urbanization prospects: 1999 Revisions*. New York: United Nations Population Division.

United Nations (2002). *World urbanization prospects: 2001 revisions*. New York: United Nations Population Division. van den Bogaard, A. E., & Stobberingh, E. E. (2000). Epidemiology of resistance to antibiotics. Links between animals and humans. *International Journal ofAntimicrobial Agents, 14*, 327-335.

Virchow, R. (1958). Scientific method and therapeutic standpoints (1849). In Rather, L. J. (Ed.), *Disease, life and man: selected essays by Rudolf Virchow* (pp. 40-66). Stanford, California: Stanford University Press.

770-776.

Western, D. (2001). Human-modified ecosystems and future evolution. *Proceedings ofthe National Academy ofSciences (USA), 98*, 5458-5465.

WHO (1995). *Executive summary. The world health report: bridging the gaps*. Geneva: World Health Organization.

WHO (2001). *The world health report 2001*. Geneva: World Health Organization.

Wiesenfeld, S. L. (1967). Sickle-cell trait in human biological and cultural evolution. Development of agriculture causing increased malaria is bound to gene-pool changes causing malaria reduction. *Science, 157*, 1134-1140.

Wilkinson, R. G. (1998). Income inequality and population health. *Social Science & Medicine, 47*, 411-412. Wilkinson, R. G. (1999). Income inequality, social cohesion, and health: clarifying the theory—a reply to Muntaner and Lynch. *International Journal of Health Services, 29*, 525-543.

Woodruff, D. S. (2001). Declines of biomes and biotas and the future of evolution. *Proceedings ofthe National Academy of Sciences (USA), 98*, 5471-5476.

Zinsser, H. (1935). *Rats, lice and history*. Boston: Little, Brown and Company.